Title

Podcasting: Podcast Launch: Simple Steps you can do to Create, Broadcast and Monetize your Podcast.

Noel Solomon

Introduction

Feeling Lost in the Shuffle

It's easy to get lost in cyber space in today's fast online business trans-actions. If you're confused and the challenge of taking your business to the next level is becoming a pale shadow of success, it's time to set up, launch, run and monetize podcast to establish your online presence and grow your business. You've more than passing interest in doing business online. Take a close look at eight essential elements of podcasting outlined in this book to grow your business.

The techniques and tips contained in this book are tailor made to assist you improve podcast presentation to achieve the ultimate business goal. Even if you don't know the first thing about podcast now, you'll learn how to set up, launch and run your own podcast in no time.

….and what is more, you will understand what you're doing because you'll Do-It-Yourself from easy step by step instructions discussed in this book. Why Not?

- Share the potential of global podcast rich heritage to grow your business?

- Save from generous income earning from business through marketing product/service with podcast.

- Salvage satisfaction of watching your business and money grow spontaneously.

- Enjoy the freedom from money management worries.

The key is to double your dollars monetizing podcasting. That is what this book is all about. You'll learn eight essential basic elements to get podcast show on the road.

- How Proper Planning Makes Perfect Podcast

- How to Launch Your Podcast

- How to Effectively Manage Your Podcast

- How to Map Out Podcast Marketing Strategies

- How to Maximize Podcast Presentation with Virtual Reality

- How to Monetize Your Podcast

- How Podcast Can Transform Small to Vast Online Business Empire

- How to Monitor Podcast Performance Progress

You could sum up podcast activity benefits with the acronym S.C.O.P.E. S.C.O.P.E. stands for the area of podcast coverage. Each letter in the acronym represents a role podcast plays in business. Here is the expanded meaning of the acronym S.C.O.P.E as it is used in this e-book.

S – Speed. Six seconds. Yes only six seconds to get your product/service message across the globe. That is pretty fast.

C – Control/Convenience. You're in control of what goes live on air online in the convenience of your office or confine of your house.

O – Organization. Nothing beats prior proper planning to prevent organization's poor performance with podcast.

P – Period/Duration of Time. Podcast cuts travel time giving you advantage to set up and run a number of episodes over short periods of time to promote product/service.

E – Economic Value. Podcast has enormous economic benefits compared to organizing conferences on physical geographical locations in strategic places around the world. Read detailed discussion on the acronym S.C.O.P.E in chapter 3. But that is not all. Podcast is evolving. There is no telling how huge podcast gains will be in a few years to come.

You think this book is not for you. That is the reason; you should definitely read it to

- Go …directly into podcast

- Get…questions directly from the target audience.

- Give…answers directly to subscribers.

Table of Contents

Sections in this Book

This book is divided into three sections. Section one, chapters 1-3 deals with podcast set up and launch. Section two chapters 4-5 dwells on podcast marketing strategies. Section three, chapters 7-8 discuss monitoring and evaluation aimed at business forecast expansion. Why choose podcast over other channels of communication?

You love to make the six figures, entrepreneurs are gloating about but don't know how. Podcast is your stepping stone to a life of luxury and convenience doing business online. You've a product/service to share and sell. You also have the gift of gab to boot!

A huge audience is waiting online provided your product/service meets the customer's physical, psychological or spiritual need. Podcast is the closest you'll ever come to addressing a mammoth audience for less with great dividends in this second awakening of internet connectivity.

You're starting out and not sure of the technicalities involved in setting up, running and monetizing podcast. This book shows you step by step from scratch to successful podcasting. Get eight essential elements to engineer better future for your business, increase cash flow, better working hours, security and satisfaction. You can discover the secret in an hour. That is how long you take to read through the content in this book to sink and set your heart on fire to improve product/service sales.

- You get hands on experience from easy to read and understand instructions in this book.
- You've access to individual personalized instruction, the easy, faster, simplified way to learn.
- You get to choose the type of podcast audio/video, topics of preference to run on your podcast calculated to meet the audience needs.

-Chapter One-

How Proper Planning Makes Perfect Podcast

There is a method of business investment which leans on Skeptical Theory. This theory digs up dirt to discover what everyone else is doing in business and doing the opposite. You should try it out.

"All those people can't be right."

The opportunity to make a fortune by reading and using tips and techniques calculated to outwit competitors online is available if you adopt the skeptical theory. However, on the ground, normal business transactions take different dimensions. Business bankruptcy and mergers continue to dominate the business community. The market plummets and you couldn't bear it if your dream business were to miserably flop. What is the secret behind successful online business stories? How can you prevent online business pitfalls?

Podcast is like politics. You don't have to be right to get into it. However, you will notice success signs which set flourishing from failing podcasting.

Seven Signs of Successful Podcaster

In computer language the acronym "GIGO," stands for "Garbage In, Garbage Out." This acronym is applicable in podcasting. You get out what you put into the podcast.

Personal satisfaction, financial stability and social status are some of the expected outcomes from putting in hours of hard work to set up and run podcast. The experience of touching base with subscribers is exhilarating. It calls for diligence and discipline to get podcast show on the road to deliver on promise weekly. Do you feel up to the challenge? Check out the following seven qualities which set successful podcaster apart from the rest of the crowd. But don't stop there; use these qualities to gauge your podcasting performance.

- Passionate About Podcast

You would rather slave to launch successful podcast than set up shop to paint, sculpture or engage in one of many creative artistic activities. The difference is in the value and premium you place on the activity.

Most people talk. Not everyone has the gift of gab to sustain fifteen, thirty, sixty minute straight talk on a topic unless you're passionate about the subject. If podcast is your scene, you engage in the activity with ease and self confidence for the love of this activity. That is what being passion about podcast is about. How does it work?

You've acquired a wealth of knowledge from researching and listening to authorities on this subject. You interact with people and read books with special emphasis in the niche. You're purpose driven to get the message across to the target audience through audio/video podcast. Read more about the difference between audio and video podcast in the next subsequent pages of this book.

- Purpose Driven Podcasting

What ideal personal, professional, financial status of business do you envisage in future? You know what you want out of life. You may not figure out how to get it yet but the blue print is there down to the last details. If you're called to business that is what you want to spend time doing daily. How to run a successful business takes different dimensions and steps, podcasting is one.

The opportunity in life to live according to the desire of your heart is available. No one and nothing can stop you from making six figures podcasting, provided it is in line with your purpose and core values in life. No matter what challenges you face, the final control over your satisfaction in life rests with you always. The money is great but it is only part of the fulfilment.

"Money only adds to your appetite, it doesn't satisfy you," Alec Titbit said. When you pursue your dreams, prepare to pay the price and happiness is guaranteed because you've a strategy to live on purpose through planning.

- Plan Podcast Strategy in Advance

Planning directs and guides you to fulfill purpose in any preferred field. Three stages of planning stand out in launching a successful podcast,

- Prior Planning
- Planning Process
- Post Planning

"Prior Proper Planning Prevents Poor Performance…," Brian Tracy observes in his book "Goals." Pre-Planning is a precondition for peak performance in sports as well as business.

You can never go wrong with proper planning of every aspect of podcast. Prior planning begins with concept development. Planning process involves selection and purchase of equipment, setting up – hardware and software links, content creation and it concludes with submission of video/audio. Post Planning takes into consideration benefits accrued from podcasting. Included in post planning is forecast for business expansion discussed in section three of this book.

In connection to developing and growing business, analyze the situation, research and gather information to assist you improve your serve. Planning is the road map that gets the business from where it is now to where you want it to be in future. Planning is also the yardstick to gauge business performance and success of the product/service in the market. It starts with self positive image.

- Project Positive Self Image

In chapter five of this book, the focus is on the importance of including virtual reality in your digital mix.

"The soul never thinks without a picture," Aristotle said. You're capable of accomplishing any task in the physical world with advance visualization of the outcome in your invisible mind through planning.

"You're not a bunch of bones in a body," Dr. Wayne Dye Self-improvement guru and bestselling author of books on the subject including Real Magic wrote. If words alone are not enough to convince you, action will demonstrate your uniqueness. You don't bother about your shadow. Yet, you stand in awe in front of a mirror to behold the beauty of your significant half. What makes the difference?

Individual personality is more pronounced in decision making. You're struggling to resolve conflict within. That should convince you of the presence of the other two aspects of human beings personalities. If negative thoughts of failure dominate your thinking to launch podcast, the project is doomed to flop from start.

However, a healthy dose of positive mental attitude will stimulate you to project positive self image in podcasting if you invest in self.

- Pay Attention to Details

Why should anyone choose to buy your product/service or do business with you? Your ability to create compelling content is clearly defined by the unique selling point proposition you project in podcasting.

How attractive is the title of the podcast? Does the topic sentence, sub headings flow and are in harmony with the body of the podcast to give you an edge over the competitor? Do you need an outline to guide and provide direction in writing the audio/video speech for the podcast?

No matter the type and length of the podcast, break it down to three basic parts introduction, body and conclusion. Pay attention to major points for discussion on the topic of discussion. Stay focused and consistent. Convey the message that move the customer to action with compelling audio/video podcast content. If these past five qualities describe your passion for podcasting, you've got what it takes to craft content that rock the listener/viewer.

- Pass On the Benefits

If you're caught in the vortex of high end tech world, you miss out passing benefits to subscribers. No subscriber wants to know you're recording the podcast in your garage as long as you pass the benefits to generate buying excitement to sell more products and offer quality services.

Promotion material, product packaging, website, are all important tools to sell the benefits through podcast. Read more about essential benefits of podcast in chapter seven of this book. Promotion is the one constant common denominator in product/service marketing strategies.

- Promote Product/Service of Preference

One world class airline was famed for its television commercial with the caption "Connecting People." The video clips of this commercial in slow motion would make anyone with emotion taste the salt of their tears. The video clips and caption remain etched in your memory long after the commercial is over.

Another priority quality of a successful podcaster seldom considered is individual satisfaction. The significance of connecting people in the commercial mentioned above is similar to the impact video podcast has on the target audience. The message of this airline commercial clearly demonstrates how you touch subscribers with video podcast with intent to grow the business. The expected ultimate outcome is to sell, sell and sell more... These are the seven signs of successful podcaster. You also need to be aware of the five priceless qualities of perfect podcast.

Five Priceless Qualities of Perfect Podcast

Business entrepreneurs read financial magazines to get views on future financial forecasts. Filthy rich folks read them for the same reason you read the newspaper to get a bird's eye view of the news round about. You read and observe the essence of the predictable and know that nobody actually predicts it. You face the danger of getting podcasting hopelessly wrong. But if you thought that, you would be wrong for two reasons.

One, these are revolutionary times. The market behaves in an unpredictable fashion. The old marketing rules are gone. This presents huge opportunity to sell more if you're fast forward in thinking of business prospects.

Two, the great thing about taking a road less travelled in podcasting is that no one can blame you if you don't know where you're going. If these ideas stretch your mind a little, I am all for it. If you have what it takes to make the idea sprout wings and fly, why not.

You've a vision. Put it to good use with a sound mission statement. Your vision serves as the foundation and stepping stone to action of the activities undertaken in doing business. It enables you to concept the business plan. However, vision goes further into directing the business enterprise. If your financial vision is focused, yet flexible, you can adjust and adopt changes in the business environment to achieve the overall objective.

You face the same challenges of launching podcast as others. No harm in giving it ago today if you're aware of the five priceless qualities of perfect podcast outlined this book talks about.

- Passion + Purpose = Satisfaction

First and foremost much of podcast work is done by you. You're passionate about the benefits of the product/service on offer. You're not just giving away your intellect. You're also giving clients and customers a head start in their preferred field of interest. That is passion. Above everything else, you're doing something that you love doing and add value to human life.

- Financial Forecasts

Institutions make a kill online with podcast. If you're interested in name dropping, turn to Forbes and read the list of world class business empires with deep roots of success on internet connectivity.

Individuals have built business empires online by forecasts of unvarying world market gloom. If the individual is right, there is round of applause for the individual's distilled wisdom and foresight. If the individual is wrong, well that is a different story altogether. Read more on Five Future Forecasts from Tracking Podcast Content in chapter eight.

- Questions and Answers (Q&A)

The second priceless quality of perfect podcast comes from listener questions challenge. You cringe at the thought that a listener would raises a question on one of your goof offs during podcast. Yet secretly you welcome the questions, suggestions and comments from listeners. The arrogant ones, even questions demanding explanations which could run past the podcast time allocation have something to offer in exchange to improve content quality and delivery.

Most listeners are under the delusion your role as a podcaster is to answer individual questions in details. Podcasters have one big fear. "Is anyone out there listening?"

A retired coal miner who spent 25 years in the pits invested his life savings online and lost the lot. Now he can't sleep at night. What can you say to him that would soothe his heart? Sympathy seems like mockery. But you believe in telling the truth that investment involves risks. How do you respond to this kind of listener and win his confidence to take another stab at online business?

"You should not put all the eggs in one basket. You should first own a house, have cash in a building society and take out insurance policies in unit trusts." Saying all this in response to the listener who has suffered financial setback is not the easiest thing to say under the circumstances. But in the end, you could save someone tuned to the podcast from sinking resources into the same financial scam.

- Delusion of Riches

Third, listeners who assume you're enormously rich from podcasting. Sure, you're doing well to host online successful podcasts. But if the listener equates you with billionaires, you need to firmly and friendly tell the person, that making more money online through podcasting is your number one priority. If you had tons of dollars starched away in the bank you couldn't use in your entire lifetime you would quit. But as it is you're in it for the money and so is the listener. This is the occupational challenge of podcasting that set you and the podcast apart from the rest of the crowd.

- Is Podcasting Full or Part Time Career?

Fourth, the jovial type of listener thinks that seventy streams of podcasts are enough to make it full time work. Podcasting is not a full time job. The listener may cry cheerily told that you've to produce the goods and work at improving the services before you can take time to talk about offering any of the two in the podcast.

Remember, the next seventy plus podcasts are going to be like the preceding seventy in most ways. You can look forward to absolute pleasure of making them because each podcast is a learning experience. Think of a different angle to present content on the product/service not covered and you've an exciting presentation in waiting.

- Brand Your Podcast

Sixth, entertainment is big business all over the world. Take a look at the figures and facts on individual celebrity income and lifestyle to understand the place and power of the entertainment industry. You hardly realize a celebrity's worth until the time of death when money matters dominate news items around the celebrity.

One revealing trend is the instant soar of sale of the musician's recordings. It happened with Elvis Presley, Michael Jackson, Mel Haggard and lately Prince. If you think of business first and bereavement second, you spot business potential in between the lines of mourning and money making.

You have a head start in numbers. Calculate the worth of celebrities in terms of brand strength range and depths, subscriber/fan base, total value and profit. Hey who said you couldn't make money from the dearly departed filthy rich personalities. Wild as this idea is, it can work if you brand it. Determine the limit to which you can make money even out of people's miseries within reason of course to save face. You got talent to make podcasting a reality. Next, pick and purchase the right equipment.

How to Pick and Purchase the Right Podcast Equipment

Purchasing equipment for podcast is a decision you take seriously. The equipment is vital to the quality and outcome of this activity. The market is flooded with new electronic gadgets competing for your attention. Buy from reputable firms with after sales service warranty.

Satisfy your budget. Get the best equipment in the market at pocket friendly price by shopping around. Don't buy on impulse. Pride in quality by choosing the latest state of the art in sound/video podcast recording equipment to give you the kind of sound and quality to pictures the target audience gets from listening to fm radio and watching internet television stations. Anything less – and the listener will move on unannounced.

You've a choice between fancy and simple basic equipment to set up. Keep in mind that the equipment meets the overall goal of the podcast. The important thing is to get the message across to potential clients and customers. You need two sets of equipment, hardware and software to run the show.

- Hardware Link

- Laptop – Any PC with audio input will work in recording audio/ video podcasts.

- Dynamic Microphone – You can get fantastic bargains on micro-phones in the market. The choice is yours provided its simple plug and play USB port with a good tripod stand.

If you plan to have a co-presenter in the show, aim for two or more microphones, have one on standby. While you're on microphone shopping spree, get USB hub to plug in the two microphones.

- Headphones – Shop for one or two good stereo headphones with-out microphone attached to them to avoid picking background sound during recording time. If you want a name try Rocket Fish headphone.

- Software Link

You need strong internet connectivity. Skype offers good quality sound and it's free and that is an advantage in cutting down cost.

Ecamm Call Record works well with Skype to record calls if you plan on including interviews during podcast. In addition, Ecamm has recording capacity to compatible to Skype.

You don't need great technical skills to manage audio podcast recording, Ecamm files are compatible. You can import and export files into the Garage Band in which you've the choice to add sound effects and music during mix down of the final sound recording from another separate audio source.

Ecamm makes editing simple and straightforward. MP3 imported files mix down well and are easy to upload to your web server FTP.

- Configuration of Website Link

Having control over your podcast is the best option to maintain quality. Own the domain name, self host, RSS feed, copyright. Nothing could be better. Check out other alternatives available in the market.

- Set Up Podcast Content Management System

Publishing your podcast on the blog with WordPress, Expression Engine or any other platform is a smart move in podcasting. You require 40-50MB per episode for uploading via FTP which is easier and faster than the normal browser. Finally, a priceless quality perfect podcast has set up fields to output RSS Page Link. Set Up Fields to Output RSS Page Link.

- RSSS Feed

Here are five stages for setting up fields for RSS feed that iTunes and Feed Burner will display on audio and video podcasts respectively.

- Episode Title

Catch the audience's attention with a good title. In chapter two you'll read about three coolest ways of grabbing audience attention in details. \

- Subtitle

This appears as description in the iTunes Web Page. Use sub titles that anchor the title of the podcast.

- Summary

Subscribers are on the go; get a well crafted summary to attract them to your audio podcast.

- Length/Duration – The shorter the episode, the better – 15 minutes is highly recommended.
- File Size

You're done with podcast set up and the RSS feed is in place. Submit content to Feed validator to correct any irregularity. Next step, submit to Feed Burner to allow more people sample your podcast with RSS or third party podcast subscription app. Here are 3 crucial steps in the submission stage.

- Submit new feed to check if the podcast options are up to date.
- Submit to iTunes Link to enjoy apples free exposure.
- Gets notification through email with a link indicating your podcast has been approved on iTunes website. What could be easy than launching a priceless perfect podcast? You don't need to lift a finger. Plug in the equipment, sit back and the equipment works fast and effectively connecting you to the global audience in seconds.

Do not get intimidated by the terminologies. They won't bite. You also don't need to memorize them to use them effectively. Most podcast equipment is plug_and_play. You can't remember the name or function. No worries. The equipment will work and that is all you need to know.

Not all is cozy setting up, launching and running your podcast. You get a bit of gloom but that is a small price to pay in comparison to the outcome. Be aware of advantages and disadvantages of podcasting.

Advantages and Disadvantages of Recorded Podcast

Advantages

- Timing – Speed is fast.
- Editing – Enjoy fantastic editing features with the latest equipment.

- Improve the quality and power of speech recording.

- Feedback to podcast. Be the first to listen and query the relevance of content. This way, you get the latitude to prepare for anticipated questions from the audience.

- Disadvantages

- Spontaneity – However much work you throw into recording podcast, the effect is less glamorous compared to live streaming of video/audio.

- Liveliness –When it comes to transmission arrangement, you're constrained to sacrifice liveliness. YouTube and iTunes facilitate and control transmission of your podcast to subscribers.

Sorry, transmission is out of your league so concentrate on creating credible content. You're getting the hang of it already huh! Not bad if you're starting from scratch. Let's wrap up this chapter with Five Ways to Create Credible Podcast Content.

Five Ways to Create Credible Podcast Content

How important is creating compelling content that drives sales through podcast is to you? Experiences of thousands who have been there, done it, indicate that making time to craft credible content pays back big time.

In some cases, the lucrative future prospect of podcasting has led many to leave paid full time day jobs to set up and run online businesses. Show me, you ask. Let's hear it from the beneficiaries.

- Yokozuna acquired impressive podcasting knowledge without leaving his home in Tokyo, Japan to give his business online presence and he has never looked back on employment.

- Michael left his managerial position as a department store in St. Paul Minnesota to engage in full time business to pursue his passion in life. Arlene, Michael's' wife and partner in running the home based store to produce and distribute chicken feeds to farmers locally and online is Godsend.

- Ann Sheila who is on a wheel chair runs service delivery business online from her home in Norway matching sponsors to disabled persons worldwide.

These three are representative of many employees turned entrepreneurs that work online and have discovered podcast as handy tool to push goods and services efficiently and effectively on the market.

The advantages of using podcast to grow small home based business to world class online business is not exclusive to anyone. You can change the world by developing content aimed at enriching other people's lives. How does it work?

Communication is the Blood line of Online Business.

Communication as a science continues to develop. Aristotle put the process down to three points which form the foundation of the frame work of communication. The basic core structure of communication revolves around speaker, speech and spectator.

Over the years communication pattern has changed from the original framework to incorporate additional two aspects which today make five essential elements of this process. However, the principles of communication remain the same. Podcast as any other model of sharing ideas, thoughts and emotions is set against the backdrop of this new model of communication structure which includes:-

- Source - Sender
- Mode/Medium
- Signal - Wireless
- Recipient – Listener/Spectator
- Destination – Global

All human relationships good or bad flourish or fail based on communication. You communicate with others all the time verbally and none verbally. The two common forms of communication are interpersonal and interpersonal. What role does these forms of communication play in podcasting? First you need to understand how each pattern works to be able to use is effectively.

Communication Patterns

Interpersonal communication is between two or more persons. Instant facial expressions, gestures, feedback are some of the outward demonstration of this type of communication pattern that takes place during dialogue. One person speaks and sends the message; the other person receives, deliberates on the message and reacts/acts.

The home, workplace and social gatherings are ideal places for interpersonal communication model. Purpose establishes quality; quality determines quantity and duration of content of your podcast.

You're looking for information to create podcast content on books through video, audio online. But you don't have time to wade through stacks and shelves of information to come up with appealing content. This book shows you the basic elements you need to know to excel in content creation. In a nutshell, three elements contribute to believable content.

- Know your Content

- Know your Audience

- Know your Method

Asking and answering questions from the audience from podcast content should assist you to narrow the episodes to a topic that meets physical, psychological and intellectual needs of the target group. Let's clothe these points with practical life examples.

- Know your Content

You communicate within self all the time. Your two natures conscious and the sub conscious, (inner and outer personality), contend with each other over what cause of action to take in decision making.

This is intrapersonal communication. In intrapersonal communication the sender and the recipient is the same. You can't pass the message you haven't thought through internally.

"You cannot step into the same river twice," one Greek Philosopher said. You cannot take back your word, that is why it's important to know what you're saying, how you're saying it and to whom you intend the message which leads to interpersonal communication.

- Know Your Audience

Who is your target audience? What needs of the audience will the podcast meet? Where is the audience? How do you intend to reach the audience?

Jesus Christ set the highest standard of effective communication. He had compassion on the multitude. In communicating with Nicodemus, a teacher of the law and the Samaritan woman Jesus changed the pattern of communication to fit the target audience needs. If you're not sure where to get information on the audience, research, read available literature on and offline. Here are three online avenues to generate information you want to know about your audience.

Quora – Visit this website to get a stream of questions posted by professionals and answers from a diverse range of respondents on the subject.

<u>Qeryz</u> - You can conduct interviews through this website to use on your podcast outlets, blog post, video/audio.

Social Networks – If you're not on Facebook, Twitter, Google+ where followers converge to compare notes your social network is wanting. However, you've no guarantee that every Tom, Dick and Harriet will respond to your question on podcast.

But a few trusted loyal friends will not let you down. You might even be lucky one of your social network friends shares a link with you to get further information. Whatever you do, social network connection should pay you back dividends. Read detailed information on social media in chapter four and five of this book.

Shape your podcast content to suit the audience and use language the audience is conversant with to achieve the overall objective of the business.

- Know your Method.

Which method video/audio podcast suit your target audience? Chapter one highlights the two commonly used methods of podcast video and audio. Make time, go over the content to choose the type which best suits you and the target audience.

- Stay Focused on Outcome

An athlete focuses on the race track focuses on winning. You've practiced, timed your performance, improved on your take off and finish line. You're good and ready to run your best time and win the medal. Podcast is no different. Your first podcast episode is your yardstick. You've put in all the work. Now it is time for delivery. Stay the mind on the ultimate outcome.

You can turn the business lifecycle around with quality presentation of content to improve product/service delivery. You know the audience level of understanding. Tailor the message to promote the product/service on podcast with Five Ways to Create Credible Content. These five ways are governed by purpose, period, people, and practical with illustrations to drive your point home.

- Purpose Driven Content

You've set the goal of increasing traffic and cash flow into the business by 5% in three months of running the podcast. This translates into doubling your income from $100-200 per month. Your aim is to excite customers to download audio/video to generate this income through podcast. It is doable with clear set standards.

- Podcast Duration

You've chosen video/audio podcast to reach the audience. Settle on podcast duration that suits your audience. If you're targeting senior citizens, your message and music in audio podcast would be chosen to match the audience preference. Use sounds of the sixties for music taste and half to forty five minute audio podcast program. Senior citizens have time to spare for listening.

If you're targeting start up business entrepreneurs online, consider using PowerPoint presentation in your video podcast. Think of using colorful slides, video clips and graphs to show business lifecycle, facts and figures variations.

- Your aim is to create linkages for future business deals with start ups. You want these visuals to emphasize details in the mind of customers to contact you for product/service delivery in future. You have the message; now meet the people half way with the content. Sample the following Real Estate Agents audio excerpt content.

Real Estate Agents

PRESENTER: If I could show you a program that could pay home loan in seven to ten months, without increasing your mortgage repayments, would it be of interest to you?

> Hello! I am Jonathan from Lake Side City Real Estate. You you've ten years or more left on your mortgage, a reasonable income and a round 40% equity in your home you could quality for this program.
>
> The benefits of paying your mortgage as quickly and cheaply are available. That is where Lake Side City Real Estate comes in.

Our mortgage optimizer plan is specifically tailor made to pay off your home loan sooner without increasing payments. You actually end up saving money and owning your own home in less than ten years.

Call in our City Headquarter Office, or at any of the branches countrywide to see if you quality. Email us now at

lakesidecityrealtors@gmail.com or visit their website for more information.

You create quality Face Book Canvas Ads to get the target audience excited about buying the product/service on offer.

"What soft drink do you prefer?" If you were asked this question at random, you would say Coca-Cola without a moment's hesitation. Coca-Cola has makes time to advertise frequently on television, radio, and online. Use the same techniques to get results with Face Book Canvas Ads.

- Back Tracking

Back tracking helps to gauge Face Book Canvas Ad performance as well as monitoring and evaluation of podcast downloads. These exercises translate into dollar value earnings.

- People Pointed Content

Use human interest illustration stories to drive your point home. People love reading about other success stories. Quote authority figures on the subject. You have no trouble with name dropping on podcast.

Be sure to give adequate information on a topic of discussion. Remember doctor's rule of thumb. Overdose is as bad as under dose. Clients and customers have other obligations to fulfill in life. Spare them information overload. When you're done scripting, put it aside for an hour or two then take a look at it again with a fresh mind. Weed out unwanted information, tweak and fine tune the final product for podcast presentation.

4. Practical Level

If you carefully plan every stage of podcast set up, launching, content presentation is practical and easy. Keep it simple with normal everyday examples to emphasize main points of discussion in the podcast. Use outline to give you guidance and direction. The outline is your road map.

Summary

When it comes to reaching a large audience online to promote your product/service, nothing works fast and effective in favor of promotion as podcast.

Chapter one examines seven significant signs of successful podcaster, explains the place of podcast in modern communication, points out five qualities of perfect podcast and concludes with five powerful ways of creating podcast content.

-Chapter 2-

How to Launch your Podcast in One Week Flat

Johannesburg, South Africa, 7:30 pm. It is Wednesday. Jenkins, one of your podcast audiences has returned from his day job. Despite the fact that he is exhausted from the pressure of work and travel, he would not miss today's podcast for the world. Jenkins has been nursing an ambition to take the plunge into full time online business for years.

"I have not been on top of things at the office these past three months," Jenkins opens up to his wife. He feels his full human potential is underutilized at the work place.

His parents wanted him to take over and run the family antique collection and selling business. Jenkins chose employment instead. He moved from one job to the next in search of satisfaction.

Jenkins was driving home from the club, one Sunday evening, his radio tuned to a local radio talk show program. The radio talk show host made discovering and using passion so simple his utter hopeless in life was put to great shame. That became his experience of the great awakening.

He realized the potential of the family business if taken to the next level. He resolved that evening to give the family business a face lift by setting up and running podcast to expand selling antiques online in addition to active participation in the family brick and mortar antique business establishment.

In three years of working hard, hand in hand with his father, the business grew to earn six figures in monthly income. Jenkins action changed the face of his family business by launching audio podcast to sell antiques online. You too can succeed in your preferred field of interest if you take seven significant steps outlined in the next topic of discussion to launch your podcast.

Seven Significant Steps to Launch Your Podcast Fast

If you're 40+ years, you've seen many changes in your lifetime. But the changes cannot be pronounced as rapid technology breakthrough of twentieth century and beyond.

The good news is technology is neutral. It is not gender bias, does not discriminate on age barrier and has no geographical location preference. You don't need college degree to set up and launch podcast. However, you do need to take seven significant steps to get the show on the road fast.

This chapter shows you how to launch successful podcast with suitable topic selection, branding, structure and format, gripping content, recording nurturing subscriber base increase.

- Suitable Podcast Topic Selection

"You're good in writing," friends have remarked time and again having read a piece you wrote and shared with them. This should be an indication that writing appeals to you more than any other artistic skills such as painting and music. How do you verify that writing is your passion in life? Put your writing talent to the test by taking three simple steps.

- Identify topic of interest on the subject.
- Set a time clock.
- Start writing for the duration of time you deem fit to hammer a good piece.

If you continue writing throughout the set time frame without hitch, give yourself a pat at the back. But don't stop there. That is only the beginning. The rest is practice, practice and practice… to perfect your writing skill. Choosing a topic for your podcast is one way of working towards the intended goal. How do you go about the process of choosing a suitable topic?

- Write down different topics that come to mind on the subject.

- Trim the list of topics you've at hand in order of importance.

- Pick on one with the greatest appeal. You could choose the title of this book as the topic sentence for your podcast.

"Podcast Launch: Seven Simple Steps to Launch a Successful Podcast." This is a killer title that would rock the target audience. You're not short on creativity in writing. Ride the pen to get the right topic. Your title choice is as good as any writer's.

- Brand Your Podcast

You establish the brand of the podcast by projecting unique selling point through two distinct qualities to make it stand out, name and logo.

- Name

What is the significance of your podcast's name? A name is important for identification purpose. Your podcast is different from the rest and so is the content and purpose. Choose a name with strong affinity to the target audience.

A good title serves as a window into the podcast. Clients are spoilt for choice. Online businesses are scrambling for a piece of iTunes pie. If the title of your podcast is not SEO friendly, you won't get noticed.

- Logo

Organizations spend money and time to develop logo. Your podcast needs a unique sign of identification in form of logo. This is what sets it apart from the rest of iTunes.

- Structure and Format of Podcast

What structure do you intend to use, audio or video? Video podcasts are attractive due to the combination of living sound and sight. Audio podcast has its place as well. However, it is not so much the medium as it is the message that carries the day.

- Frequency

Be consistent in maintain the target audience to build confidence on the product/service. If you schedule weekly podcast, keep to it. Deliver on promise.

- Duration

The duration of the podcast depends on your ability to use allocated time to the maximum. 15, 30, 50 minute segments are popular. Shorter episodes are within attention span of most listeners. No one has the time for stories in one podcast episode. Unless the narrative is used as lead story for opening, it would fall flat on its face in the podcast and derail you progress. Split the topic into segments over duration of time say three months but maintain time slots and continuity of the topic of discussion.

For example in the first series of your podcast presentation on attracting audience attention you could use these titles in the series.

- Story Opening

- Staggering Statistics

- Show with Photos

- State Facts with Visual Aid

There is no monopoly on titles, come up with original unique titles for your brand of podcast.

- Compelling Podcast Content

Content is the heartbeat of podcast. All other activities associated with this activity come a distant second in the list of priority. You've purpose. You've worked on podcast brand. Structure and format are in place. Content crowns it all, because without content, none of these steps make podcast successful.

Brainstorm. Put down podcast topics of interest in writing. If you're podcasting about starting home based online business, choose topics on the subject that are a must read and must watch video podcast. Write down and spread the series out in different episodes. Example if you're podcasting on writing.

You could settle for "7 Reasons Why Writing is the Best Career Choice of a Lifetime," as the title. Break the episodes down into segments with topics reflecting the main title. Run the first three episodes of this title on,

- Writers

- Writing

- Written Word

Script

Write down the content word for word especially the introduction to get off to a good start. Scripted content will guide and give you direction during presentation. Do you need an outline to assist in covering the topic adequately? If so, put one in place.

Bullet points assist to emphasize sub titles on the script. Ad lib to give it flavor, yet keep your eyes on the ultimate goal.

- Recording Podcast Content.

 Recorded video or audio has great advantages. You've control over the content that gets transmitted to the intended audience. Not to mention the opportunity and time to get the best episode out through editing the content to size and flow. Time the duration and the segments in the episode to match service providers allocated time frame.

Technical aspects of putting together video or audio podcast differ significantly but not the message. Chapter one summarizes the kind and type of equipment you need. There is no harm in rereading it again.

- Nurture and Increase Your Audience

You've done all the ground breaking work. The podcast is up and running. The challenge is to maintain and increase your fan base. If you create interactive and engaging audio/video content, half the battle is won. You can attract good following by giving away incentives.

- Website – WordPress has premium quality with high speed running capacity. You can upload sections of your book on the blog with ease.

- Encourage the audience to participate, conduct surveys, and get feedback as you keep an eye on podcasts analytics.

- Spread the word on your podcast launch through social media. Encourage subscribers to rate your podcast, get reviews. These are great avenues to get your product/service noticed as well as give your podcast endearing online presence. How do you grab attention of the audience in podcast? This is the next topic of discussion in this chapter.

Three Coolest Ways to Grab Audience Attention

"Purpose Determines Content," is one of the principles of communication. You have the liberty to choose the title and topic of podcast. There is no magic wand in this exercise. Don't wait for the topic to nudge you out of reverie. It won't. You've purpose and set goal to fulfill. Your brain will steer you towards the right direction to pick on a killer title and topic of choice for the podcast.

Purpose dictates the message and leads to suitable choice of title and topic sentence in the podcast. Asking questions stimulates the brain to explode with unique titles and topic sentences on the subject matter.

Online business flourishes on websites and social media potential to attract and monetize your podcast. Read exclusive monetizing podcast in chapter three. How do you maintain interest of traffic that pay your website, social media page a visit? Here are three coolest ways to grab the attention of visitors long enough to turn them into clients.

1. Free Offers

If your inbox is not overflowing with giveaway emails, you're on the wrong side of the internet. You get notifications online on just about everything free, eBooks, consultations, videos, coupons, or downloadable.

"This offer is only available until midnight." In a separate email,

"This is it. The free e-book you've been waiting for is finally out. Click here to download your copy of (*Title of e-book*) today." If you're done with advertising emails, you get this one

"Our books are free, get your copy today." This announcement is tagged with the book title and tagline.

In some cases, the consultation giveaway is subtle.

"This month…JK Rawlings history of rejection, consider the 'writer's bible,' get answers to questions…" Joan Dempsey

How would you like this invite?

"Hear all about ….and more – get paid opportunity by listening to once a week (Insert Title of your Podcast.")

"… We're launching a new podcast this month that details….." You would also want to discover more from SocialMediaExaminer.

Here are …quick links to iTunes, Stitcher, RSS feed.

…Watch this video on your iPhone."

Giveaways are the norm rather than the exception marketing strategy. Get your foot inside the marketing door of clients with an incentive and you've access to a great deal more...

The title of this e-book highlights the importance of benefits of podcast. This is a subtle way of getting noticed by potential clients. Shower them with freebies in exchange for email correspondence.

2. Contests

Contests generate excitement as well as engage online participation from a wide spectrum of the target audience. How would do you gauge artistic skill such as writing without entering a contest? Contests provide equal opportunity for individuals to showcase their talents by winning the prize. But it is also a great way to get noticed.

Contests have deadlines. This puts the squeeze on time and urgency to get in. There are many contests going on as there are contestants and contest organizers in different fields. Writing, Sweepstakes, Referrals and Photo/Video contests are some of the most popular ones on demand. Run one or two in your podcast, sit back and watch what happens to traffic flow into the website.

3. Brick and Mortar Establishments

Brick and mortar establishment businesses run on physical traffic. This is the secret behind art exhibitions, book fairs and agricultural shows. Online business may have put a dent on brick and mortar business establishments but it can't put them out of business altogether.

Great businesses deals are transacted on physical locations. Nothing beats spread out books on benches outside physical bookshop to attract potential buyers. Supermarkets, the main avenue for human beings nourishment are overflowing with food stuff on display on physical locations. Despite online popularity, physical location is a good avenue to lure clients to buy your product/service. The combination of both provides fantastic business opportunity for advancement and growth. Jenkins in chapter one, is a good example of combining online with brick and mortar establishment efforts to grow business.

These three are by no means the only ways to attract audiences; craft innovative ways in your preferred field of doing business and you stand to make mileage podcasting.

Summary

If your business is not yielding the benefits you deserve, let the experts handle technical part of podcast to allow you concentrate on generating content to launch and monetize your podcast.

There is no surer way of cutting costs, speeding production and improving reliability of online business than by taking seven significant steps to launch podcast and choosing 3 coolest ways to grab the audience attention. This chapter explains step by step activities methods that lead to launching podcast in a week flat.

-Chapter 3-

How to Effectively Manage Your Podcast

One Stop Software Solutions (OS3) started in 2005 as a consultancy and business service to assist new entrepreneurs start and build solid foundation in business online. OS3 offered free management services and developed user friendly software for the small band of 7 members that first signed up for the program.

This pilot project revolved around podcasts/software development by individual entrepreneurs. The first phase of the project involved orientation, identification of products/services. OS3 provided consultancy and advised on pricing policy while member entrepreneurs spent time on awareness creation of the different products/services on the house. OS3 established guideline for evaluation of progress reports and success of the different businesses.

- Progress Evaluation and Upgrade

In seven months of operation, OS3 undertook management and planning assessment of its operation and came up with modification recommendations to the original model. This assessment led to upgrade OS3 service delivery program.

Included in physical involvement to oversee the progress of member businesses, the management also set up to run a series of podcasts to meet the growing demand of member organizations. The seven member entrepreneurs were OS3 first subscribers to the podcast.

OS3 members had the privilege to download podcasts and use them for reference in time of need. This change in model of OS3 program was justified in cost effectiveness and in building future working collaboration working relationships.

Success stories of the small start up businesses achieving set objectives with assistance from OS3 became the organization's stepping stone to get new clients into the project through reference by member entrepreneurs.

- Future Prospects

Today, One Stop Software Solutions continues to work with 70+ small startup business entrepreneurs generating reasonable revenue income and increasing profit margin from consultancy service delivery. This is one kind of management associated with podcasting. Payment and production of goods are two other management opportunities covered in subsequent chapters in this book.

In this chapter, the focus is on the overall podcast management strategy. This chapter shows you how to manage your podcast effectively. Here, the discussion on management draws on One Stop Software Solutions experience to make good its promise. The principles are the same across the board with variation on specific areas of management of podcasting. What was the secret of One Stop Software Solutions?

S.C.O.P.E: Podcast Wonder Working Acronym you read about in the introductory section of this book and six subtle techniques in this chapter will take the mystery out of learning how to manage podcast effectively with confidence.

It may seem odd at first – the idea of speaking to remote audience online. You might think you need a private teacher. The steps in this book show you with simple words and practical illustrations, what to do when, where and how to it from scratch.

How do you know that you're doing it right? You've plenty of practice time with short simple messages. You get confidence to know how to plan and prepare podcast. You can tell the right way and quality of sound/video when you get it right by pairing them with four subtle techniques to manage podcast effectively.

S.C.O.P.E: Podcast Wonder Working Acronym

Introductory remarks to this book briefly touch on S.C.O.P.E. Here is recap of the sentiments expressed on this acronym to bring you up to date in discussing podcast management. S.C.O.P.E. signifies area of podcast coverage. Letters in the acronym stand for and represent roles of each activity the letter represents.

You'll also be introduced to seven fundamental functions of podcast management in connection with the use of S.C.O.P.E to explain the task at hand. These seven functions are represented by each letter in the word PODCAST. Each of the seven letters in the word P.O.D.C.A.S.T covers the full spectrum of the colors in the rainbow which signifies completeness of the process. How do you weave these two sentimental acronyms with set up, launch to run podcast? Here is a breakdown and explanation of each letter in the word P.O.D.C.A.S.T.

P- Planning

O - Organization

D - Directing

C - Controlling

A - Asking and Answering Questions

S - Structure and Format

T - Techniques

Seven Fundamental Functions of Podcast Management

- Planning

Nothing compares to careful planning for the success of any business undertaking. Business, sports, self improvement revolve around planning to determine the course of direction and action for future expansion or demise of the task at hand. You got a healthy dose on "How Prior Planning makes Perfect Podcast," in chapter one. Effective planning does the following three things to business.

- Clears Clutter
- Crystallizes the Vision
- Cuts down on Cost

There is no stoppage time in planning to succeed in podcasting, whether in setting up, content creation, recording the material, launching and submission. Planning starts with a written document many call business plan but does not end there.

This is an ongoing process throughout the business lifecycle. Strategic planning begins with a vision. You've a vision for business? Process it in the mind by asking and answering three simple questions to make the vision clear and fall into place.

- Where are you on the scale of doing business?
- What is your destination?
- How do you get there?

If you adequately address these three simple questions, half the work of running a successful podcast which leads to organization development is done.

- Organization

Organization is your ability to blend professionalism and human potential through structured tasks to get the job done. Organization includes dealing with human resources of different temperaments in a large institution.

The secret is to determine how to accomplish assigned tasks by individuals in the organization. Your work is to coordinate and facilitate the process. Think of organization in podcasting as a series of activities. You've set objectives to accomplish within given time frame.

- Identify the activities in categories
- Allocate time for specific tasks.

Strengthening the foundation of organization structure leads to creation of linkages with other organizations in the industry and individual consumers of the product/service. Structure defines the organization which in turn gives guidance and direction to the business.

- Directing

Think of different ways of motivating people under your supervision at the workplace. Motivation is "motive in action." However if you're the proprietor, doubling up as CEO, manager, clerk, finance advisor, motivation takes a different dimension and requires a lot more than thinking of ideas.

You're dealing with three aspects of the human life physical, psychological and spiritual in the case of individual motivation. Leave out any of these three aspects and the institution/individual takes a nose dive into oblivion. You must be on the driver's seat of your life to direct and take activities of the podcast to the next level. This is what control is all about.

- Controlling

Your role in the process of maintaining the organization on course is to control its performance to influence outcome. You want nothing less than quality podcasting. Craft, record and transmit credible content that sets tongues wagging long after subscribers have downloaded and used the content.

- Ask and Answer Questions

Five priceless qualities of perfect podcast covered in chapter one details the importance of asking and answering listeners' questions. Brush over it.

Picture this. A lady listener calls you on Skype and talks for three quarters of an hour. No doubt, she is brilliant. She wants to sink her savings into online pyramid scheme. You explain, cajole, beg but there is a limit to the time you can spend saving someone from the consequences of her folly. She might call you names, jump a few, but you've the obligation to uphold priceless perfect podcast. Stick with it.

- Structure and Format

One of Seven Significant Steps to Launch Your Podcast discussed in chapter two touches on structure and format. This proposition is also mention in chapter one on Podcast: Parting Shot between tradition and modern business enterprises.

If you're undecided whether to use video or audio podcast refer to these two sections for clarity on structure and format. These two sections explain and examine the pros and cons of video and audio podcast structure and format. Be sure to check them out.

- Techniques to Stimulate Podcast Success Steam

"Well began is only half done," a Chinese proverb says. You've made time, spent energy and resources to set up, build your podcast from scratch. All the effort would amount to nothing if you don't manage the podcast to run well and on course.

Managing your podcast effectively involves seven subtle techniques discussed in the next topic. This section takes you through five podcast set up fields before you learn seven steps which can make or break your podcast.

The sentiments discussed in chapter on "How to Pick and Purchase the Right Podcast Equipment," cannot be over emphasized to reassure you that podcast coast is clear. Let's set sail with five set up fields.

Five Podcast Set Up Fields

- Identify Podcast Category

Smart phone, iPod, iPhone, tablet and personal computer are established avenues for podcasting in the market.

You can also set up podcast platform with WordPress Blog Post. WordPress blog is easy to use, simply add new category "Podcast." Be sure to install audio player in plugins field if you've not done so already.

Choose recording software from a range of software available in the market to suit your taste. If you fancy boldness working with recording facility and editing content, go for it. Next,

- Obtain the domain name
- Establish a Feedburner and you're set to submit your podcast. Visit the Feedburner to get information.

Gmail account works fine. Take the liberty to choose a different account if you so wish. Paste the podcast feed URL in the blank field provided. Then, identify the feed address and Feed title. Configure the podcast to allow Feeedburner list the podcast in iTunes and you've a done deal.

2. Record Audio/Video

In recording audio or video podcast, here are six items to pay attention to.

- Podcast Title – Brand or Blog name in addition to "podcast," is adequate. Tagline gives the added advantage to specify your niche for SEO.
- Talent Name – Your name forms part of the brand.
- Podcast Sub Title – One or two short descriptive lines on the podcast.

- Podcast Summary – Summary contains podcast episode material in a nutshell.

- Art Work – Logo for identification. Make it attractive to the audience.

- Record the Podcast – You've access to simple down to earth instructions to carry out this exercise. Refresh your memory with details of activities on recording podcast in chapter two.

- Share Your Podcast.

You've a brilliant product/service idea for prospective clients and customers. How would they hear it unless you submit the podcast through iTunes and video podcast service provider? Take these three steps to share your podcast.

- Sign up for iTunes account.

- Select Podcast tab in iTunes

- Submit Podcast

- Upload with MP3 Audio File

Review the information on MP3 audio files discussed early in this book.

- Start an Account

- Select Settings - Key in required details.

- Save

- Publish the podcast by selecting advanced publisher.

In this era of Do-It-Yourself (DIY), podcasts is easy to set up if you've the right gear for audio/video.

Pros

- Know the message. Presentation is your creativity to interact with the audience

- Audio podcast support audio alone.

- Audio podcasts have a wide range of avenues and can be translated into different languages for distribution to reach a wider audience.

- Preview – Go over the material to make sure it matches the overall objective of the business.

Cons

- Audio podcasts are suited for easy to listen and understand and not complicated subjects that require use of sight.
- Audio podcasts are limited in scope as SEO does not always pick them up.
- Video podcast take up chunks of space in the computer memory chip

Six Subtle Techniques to Manage Your Podcast Effectively

"He who aims at nothing hits it all the time," the old adage says. In connection with marketing product/service, "If everyone is your customer, no one is your customer." The purpose for participation in the game of darts is to hit bull's eye. When you do, it is game shot. Take a look at the seven subtle techniques to enable you manage podcast effectively.

- Define Marketing Strategy

Podcast showcases your brand and promotes product/service. Striving to make sale, breaking even in business and increasing profit margin are accrued benefits of this exercise.

In your comprehensive plan to start the business you put down marketing research as part of management process. Your business deserves the best. Management is your entry ticket to the business community dance hall. How do you manage podcast on an ongoing basis? Ask pointed questions to get answers which solve management matters.

When you know the target market, you've the ability to improve focus and marketing ability of the product/service through podcast promotion techniques.

Whether you set to run business to business, business to individual podcasts, keep the benefits at the forefront of marketing strategy.

- Distinguish Your Podcast from the Rest.

What makes your podcast different from the rest? Your podcast is fashioned in tune with original business blueprint. The business plan is your North Pole reference point. Refer to it from time to time to stay on top of the game.

Annual revision of the business plan points in the right direction to backtrack earnings. You draw lessons from subscriber's feedback, sales and traffic flow from visits on the website to make adjustments in specific areas which need further research and new material injected into the program. This is the move Jenkins took to turn around the family business.

- Develop Superior Customer Service Care

No customer. No cash flow. No business. The aim of any business activity is to deliver product/service on promise. If you set out to run one podcast weekly make time to deliver on promise.

- Death of Start Up Businesses

80% of start up businesses will fizzle out within six months of operation. Only 20% of new businesses see the light of day. These statistics are backed by proven records from years of research.

Podcast is touted as the bloodline of most modern business enterprises. Gauging the business performance requires you to backtrack and discover business cash flow, potential and problems. You've a good list of subscribers to fall back on for feedback to carry out this exercise.

You know podcast is not meeting its intended objective from low sale turnover of products collecting dust in the warehouse months after production. Be sure to track down the stumbling block in the system to move the product/service fast and efficiently in order to scale up profit margin.

- Draw Lessons from Past Experience

"Experience is the best teacher," the old saying goes. You can learn a great deal from past blunders if you keep trying with eyes fixed on the future business ultimate goal achievement. Listen to other podcasts in your niche with understanding. Set to do it better. Keep up to date with new developments in the industry, new trends; events to enable you forecast future business expansion.

"If you can't beat them, join them." You've tried everything in the book yet your sales remain low. What are other podcasters doing to clock the six figures that you're not? Discover the secret behind the success of other podcasters then set to model it to your podcast advantage.

- Deal Directly with Audio/Video Service Providers

Anyone can podcast, but no one can do it better than you. There is no age limit, no geographical location boundary imposed, and the capital investment on equipment to set up and run podcast is affordable. However, if you don't deal directly with audio/video service providers, the process is slow and stunted.

Summary

Rapid rate of change in the use of computers for domestic and business purposes through internet connectivity has changed the face of communication industry. This is the focus of chapter three.

In choosing a suitable title for the podcast, you're working towards branding the podcast. In addition, to structure and format, you create compelling content that will nurture and grow the audience and business. Chapter three explains how these goals are achieved.

Now is the time to trade valuation of old for new business methods of communication with potential to monetize on gains from podcast performance. It's time to tap into the potential of podcast now, not tomorrow.

-Chapter 4-

How to Map Out Marketing Strategies through Social Media

Highways to the stars explorers used accurately to navigate their way are today "mapped," out by modern technology devices.

When a passenger aircraft is held or diverted due to poor visibility in bad weather condition, it means a great deal more than missed appointments for the passengers. It translates into heavy loss for the operating company of the aircraft because modern high performance aircraft is kept flying extra mileage with the same earning operating costs capacity. That is the reason there is pressure to develop fully reliable blind landing facilities in such events. Deliberate over space exploration scenario in connection with online business. How can you Make the Most of Social Media Marketing Strategy in Podcasting?

"Yesterday is already a dream and tomorrow is only a vision. But today well lived makes yesterday a dream of happiness and every tomorrow a vision of hope."

This anonymous quote illustrates three periods of human life. These three periods also signify online business lifecycle. Without the past, there would be no present, and without the present, the future is nonexistent.

In section one, chapters 1-3 the discussion tilts towards audio podcast. This second section, chapters 4-6, gleans on the place and power of video podcast. The concluding chapters 7 and 8 blend the role of audio and video podcasting with marketing strategy in growing your business. This chapter presents Four Mandatory Marketing Strategies, Dozen Face Book Instant Articles and Six Simple Ways to Set Up Quality Face Book Canvas Ads.

Four Mandatory Social Media Marketing Strategies

Mention food and images of a mother feeding her baby, celebration and feasting during important occasion such as weddings and funerals come to mind. The cultural centrality of food consumption and demand for supply is ever increasing. That is the reason why food has some of the most significant associations in society.

The need for nourishment provides great demand for supply of food stuffs by small scale farmers who are the backbone of agricultural sectors in most countries. You don't university degree in agriculture to make a kill out of farm produce. Here is how.

You have podcasting knowledge to communicate and provide farmers with a platform to sell produce. You also have technical knowhow to assist these farmers produce quality horticulture to meet the local and international market needs. What more can you ask for?

You need to bring the local farmers together under one umbrella. Your work is to facilitate, between the market and farmers. Farmers get to sell produce to ready market, you've identified through research and members of the group subscribe to your podcast and download content on smart phones.

Another opportunity available to extend your podcasting activities in agriculture and influence outcome is through radio talk show to reach a wider audience in the local market. This avenue opens doors to supply brick and mortar establishments with produce for sale to customers. These ideas are pregnant with future expansion of business in the agricultural sector. The ideas are real. Here are four tips and techniques to stimulate your podcasting steam.

- Clear Clutter

It is easy to sign up for new and exciting free give away online. Within no time, your inbox is reeling under information overload, most of which you've not had time to open and read, let alone have any idea on content of information contained therein. This is not because of lack of interest; rather the squeeze on time occasioned by demanding obligations in life makes it difficult but not impossible to attend to all emails that arrive into your inbox daily. How do you remedy the situation? Do it now! Keep up to date with your correspondence by making time to read emails as they arrive to avoid cluttering your inbox.

If you don't value the contents, dispose of unimportant emails. Make time once a week, a month, or whatever duration is convenient to clean up your inbox. Delete data that is taking up valuable space or move it to a secondary storage facility to free space in your personal computer.

Your computer runs well and fast on good size memory. Two, you're able to sort out stuff and deal with the most pressing issues at hand. Three, if you can clear email clutter; you can do the same in other areas of your life.

- Check Out Links

Check out links associated with your podcast, including social networks and decide what messages to keep and which ones need to go. Trim down the list of emails and information to make it easy to receive only what you need and can readily use.

You've a million followers on Face Book. That is great. But do you have the time to respond to each of them? Who gets first class priority response? What messages do you keep for future reference? You alone have answers to these questions. Address them to stay on course podcasting.

- Combine Social Media with Google Analytics

Social Media with Google Analytics present a good picture of business performance progress online. Use both alternatively to get customer information that leads to making modifications and building a solid foundation for your business expansion in the future. Seek to excite the customer to spend on the product/service through podcasting.

- Change Settings, Features

You change clothes, sitting arrangement in the house and diet all the time. You should also change settings of the podcast to match with the times. Introduce new exciting features to give podcasting a new spin with photos, music, sound effects as you add value and vitality to the podcast.

If you're not on Face Book, you're out of phase with social media. The reason is simple. Numbers don't lie. Statistics show and you know you're either on social media or missing out in business action around the world.

Whether you're in business for kicks or keeps, buyers determine market price of your goods/services from marketing strategies. How will potential clients know about your product/service unless you tell them? No one is going to break down your warehouse door to get goods. You take the goods to customers using different channels of promotion.

Audio listeners take podcasts with them jogging, sightseeing and camping. Create user friendly content for consumers to use in the field, office and social gatherings. You want to experience business growth through podcasting. Participate actively in the game. Where do you get ideas for podcast?

- Thoughts Have Wings.

You can influence others with your thinking. If you were to concentrate on another person seated in a room with you, without the person noticing, the result would amaze both of you. When you observe keenly, the person gradually becomes restless and finally turns to look in your direction. Simple – yet it works all the time. Try it on podcast.

This positive demonstration shows how thoughts generate mental energy which can be projected from your mind to the consciousness of subscribers to your podcast. Do you realize how much of your success and happiness in life depends on influencing others through podcast? It is important that the target audience understands your point of view to be receptive to the message of your proposals? How many times have you wished there were ways you could use to impress another person – get across to the person with a new idea?

It is now scientifically proven that thoughts can be transmitted, received, retrieved and understood by others. Tales of miraculous accomplishments of the mind by the ancient philosophers are now known to be fact-not fable. The methods used for this kind of exercise can be intentionally used in podcasting.

You produce goods for sale to satisfy customer needs. Service delivery has different distinct characteristics from products. Service delivery unique characteristic takes the form of the sense of sound.

Pricing Policy determines the value attached to the product/service.

Manufacturers store goods in warehouses for safe keeping and points of contact but the aim is to move the goods fast to wholesale, retail outlets and make the goods accessible to clients and customers in the open market. How do you accomplish this task?

- Hunt for Greater Return On Investment (ROI) with Podcasting

There are over 10 million smart phones in the market. That is a huge business opportunity to explore with audio podcast. But that is not all. You don't have to go for broke to monetize the business through podcasting. You can tap into this vast treasure with basic equipment and reap great benefits by creating compelling audio podcast content.

You need passion and persistence to get the message across if you expect quick turnaround income. The only tried, tested and trusted way to gauge the success of podcasting is to learn by doing. So, is everyone running online business keen on ROI from podcasting? How can you avoid financial setback and prevent your business from taking a nose dive? Three essential elements ensure podcasting achieves overall business goals. The three include but not exclusive to,

- Research and document market variation.

- Acquire hands on podcasting knowledge and skills.

- Discover what the competitor is doing to succeed and do it better.

The value of setting up, launching successful podcasting is demonstrated by the achievement of thousands of entrepreneurs who have taken their businesses to the next level with this exercise. You can do the same.

Jenkins, of Johannesburg, South Africa is the proud owner and CEO of a thriving online business selling antiques. You remember Jenkins in chapter two on "How to Launch your Podcast in One Week Flat."

"We've more orders for antiques than we can supply," Jenkins observes. "Our worldwide demand for antique items has outstripped the supply a hundred fold in seven years," he adds. This family business has opened up stores across the globe with over 300 employees on the payroll," Jenkins proudly says. But Jenkins is not the only beneficiary of podcasting.

Daniel J. Smith started podcasting part time while on day job three years ago. Six months later having acquired skills and knowledge in podcasting, he reported,

"I was promoted to manage the company communications department at La Moure, N.D." This great achievement is traced back to Smith's tireless efforts to walk on a road less travelled by employees in the firm.

Sandra Frost, of Bexhill on Sea, England was stuck in a low paying television and radio repair work for years before starting her own, setting up and running podcast offering the services to potential clients in the local community. Sandra is currently running electronics training online and weekly podcast as well as supervising a group of seven apprentices in her home town repair workshop.

"I am working six, down from 30 hours a week compared to when I started off. My income has tripled in the last three years and so is the take home pay from the day job," she says.

These three among thousands have taken their businesses to greater heights of prosperity with audio/video podcasting. Why not you? Yours is the next success story.

Dozen Deals of Face Book Instant Articles Marketing Techniques

Increase in popularity of Face Book social media network makes this platform lucrative destination to tap into 8 billion jackpot users. You can't afford to miss out on this emerging market gem. How do you position your business online with Face Book Instant Articles? The presence of social media outlets and the fact that you can publish articles on Face Book alone presents huge benefits for business development and growth.

The average age of your audience in Face Book includes the greatest potential clients with the highest purchasing power for the product/ service. Here are a dozen deals that will pay you top dollar value from using Face Book Articles.

You can publish up to ten articles down from the initial requirement of 50 articles. That is a big reduction. What steps do you need to take to set up and publish these ten articles? Here are seven steps you'll never regret taking.

Seven Silent Steps for Using Face Book Instant Articles to Boost Profit Margin

- Sign up Made Easy

This is your show in your own time and speed.

- Speed – You'll be amazed. Online equipment speed is so fast you hardly notice. You're in business in less than five minutes in the process of signing up.

- Safety – This is part of service delivery offered by service providers. It is not always guaranteed. You play a big role in ensuring safety standards are maintained online by keeping your end of the bargain with a secure secret code and pass word to your email, Face Book, bank account and work platforms to facilitate safety precautions.

- Security – If you've Face Book account, half of the job is done. You're good and ready to enable instant articles on Face Book page.

Here are three steps that will get you up and running instant articles on this platform in no time.

- Step 1 – Sign Up

Answer a few simple questions and away you go. You save time, energy and resources. It's also convenient and comfortable. No one is looking over your shoulders to point out mistakes. Who wants to know that you're slow as a snail or fast as gazelle in the wild signing up online?

- Step 2 - Set up Article Space

Signing up for Face Book account takes little time. Spend more time getting to know your way around and how to navigate the new online terrain. But once you've got the hang of it, enabling instant articles steps fall in place instantly. You've a number of actions to set on course for this exercise once you locate instant article menu.

Quick start guideline is the handy tool that takes you through the steps quickly and easily to use this facility. Here is a list of items you've access to instant article menu:

Page Manager Apps enables articles and styles compatibility to iOS Android.

URL – Remember that in section one in setting and launching podcast.

Templates – These predefined outlays allow you to create fantastic features that help in customizing, tailor made article on Face Book

RSS Feed – Refresh your memory with discussion on this topic from section one.

Monetizing your article on Face Book topic discussion is given prominence in chapter six. Be sure to read and understand it. In the meantime,

- Step 3 – Submit Article for Review. You need feedback from Face Book team to give you the go ahead or make adjustments in line with editorial standards of this platform. Face Back team gets back to you in 24-48 hours to go ahead and publish the articles or make corrections
- Set up Space

- Start with Quick Start Guideline

Quick start guidelines provide you with the tools and necessary instructions on matters of links to attend to at the beginning. You do this once for all.

- Clear Your URL

- Set up RSS Feed

- Configure the page to Monetize. All the above three areas are covered in details in section one of this book. You should be aware of their functionality if you read the section well. In case of any lingering doubt, go back and reread to section one for further information and clarity.

Publishing articles on Face Book is part of the wider promotion scheme to increase profit margin in the business. Setting the right configurations in the initial stages of launching your podcast pays big time in the long run. Do it right now!

Your audience network list gets you through the door, but you've to push the door open wide with good article content to attract clients and enlist customers to buy the product/service on offer. You're ahead of the competitors by following these rules of thumb. .

Be sure your articles are optimized for Face Book. Ensure the articles have no typos, no glaring grammar and spelling mistakes which put off readers and derail the purpose. Explore all available ways of publishing instant articles. Select the best, leave out the rest to take advantage of monetizing the articles to pay you back big dividends.

- Brand Your Articles

You're a brand, so is your business. Face Book instant articles should reflect and point in that direction. The steps to brand your business and instant articles could be different but the ultimate aim is the same – to monetize podcasting. Call it increase profit margin, monetize, or any good sounding words to describe the process, the bottom line in doing business is to make money. Refer to the process of branding discussed earlier in this book again, if you need to refresh your memory with the information.

- Set up Email Alerts

How will your Face Book fans, friends and foe know about the new product/service you just launched with a fifteen minute weekly podcast? Shout it from the rooftops with email alerts. This book takes the hard work out of your hands to allow you to write and publish instant articles.

- Check for Errors and Rid articles of flaws

First impressions are significant. You're hitting the road running with a new product/service, post instant articles on Face Book that are error and plagiarism free. Leave nothing to chance.

Clean up and polish instant article before publishing it on the public domain. You don't want tongue lashing and bad feedback reputation that could spoil your reputation online from common writing mistakes when you're in a hurry.

- Preview Articles on Face Book Apps

Previewing your article prior to publishing is comforting. This exercise gives you control of what is published on your Face Book page. You've access to Face Book apps for iOS Android devices with instant articles facility. Use all available avenues to give the product/service greater appeal and wide S.C.O.P.E of reaching the audience.

Do your best to edit, tweak, and fine tune the article to the required standard for marketing. Whatever changes, you make should add and make the article well rounded to attract organic traffic to your website, podcast, blog post. Let your instant articles stand out and shine on the line in the industry.

- Submit Articles

You've read the article umpteenth time and satisfied with the masterpiece. You've the required ten articles to set sail with this ship. You do no more than submit the first instant article for Face Book team review and approval and the rest as they say follow suit.

- Get Feedback to Assist Clean Up Writing for Publication.

You'll get notification in 24-48 hours on instant articles from Face Book team. If the articles are approved go ahead and publish. Article disapproval is not rejection. It means sharpening the writing.

Get Published. That is what every dedicated writer aims to achieve in writing. How do you do that with instant articles on Face Book? Here are seven must do things to clean up your instant article.

- Rid your writing of redundant cliché's. Cliché's are a sign that your writing needs more work. Tighten the sentences to make original masterpiece and not a carbon copy of tired old phrases.

- Use available soft ware to smoke cliché's out in a flash and to expose sections where cliché's are hiding in the writing. Locate and replace cliché's with fresh words. Removing redundancies breathes new life and vitality into writing.

- Review your work. Make specific use of situation or setting for inspiration. Give your work a new spin and it will catch the listener's ear in audio podcasting.

- Relieve your manuscript of overused words that clutter your work and clog the system of flow with passive instead of active voice. You wind up with second class descriptions starting with "ing," verbs and conjunctions if you use passive verbs.

- Remake your writing with variety of sentences, short and sharp, medium and long. If possible, enlist a friend to read and give you a second opinion on the writing. If you think the friend is out to pick on trivial mistakes, so be it provided the writing is clean and crisp to read. Sentences like "He turned the car back," seem harmless. Use direct wording in sentence construction, "He turned the car," to turn on your writing charm.

- Repeated words and phrases show up in unexpected parts of writing all the time. Avoid putting readers to sleep with meaningless words and phrases. Tools for cleaning up your writing are godsend. Use one or multiple tools to get the writing liveliness. Feedback from Face Book team or friend should point you in the right direction for improvement.

- Have you ever wondered why some instant articles on Face Book bore you to near death, while others you can't stop reading until you're done? Interesting articles, books don't just happen. Writers make them happen. You've talent and skills. Use the two to tidy up your work and give it fresh appeal.

- Revision and rewriting instant articles becomes easy using editing tools to improve the quality and make it stand out in the crowd.

Whatever your motivation for writing instant articles on Face Book, make the exercise worth the audience time reading it to get excited about purchases. These dozen deals on writing will land you top dollar in monetizing instant articles on Face Book from clicks in addition to setting up Face Book Canvas Ads.

Six Simple Steps to Set Up Quality Face Book Canvas Ads

Times change and technology is fast forwarding the pace to new unknown age. You're not sure how to tap into the vast majority of Mobile Face Book users to expand your business. Stop doubting and start working to create quality ads on Face Book Canvas. The technology for doing this is available.

If you're techno savvy, you've either heard or used this new online advertising facility. How do you create face Book Canvas Ads page? In the wake of modern technology new ways and opportunities for doing business have come up for would be users. Face Book Canvas Ads is the latest tool targeting the huge following on this platform. These are your potential clients and customers.

Take advantage of the numbers on this platform to expand your audience market base. But, it gets better. This service is FREE to use if you're into freebies and Face Book advertisement costs freaks you out. The advantages associated with expansion of your business through Face Book Canvas Ads are many

- The ad takes up a good portion of the page leaving no room for any competing items to be slotted on the page.

- Fast loading time makes Face Book Canvas ads easily accessible and readily available to use.

Here are six ways you can make the most of Face Book Canvas Ads to scale up your online business.

- Videos and Text Make Formidable Marketing Strategy Force

Squeeze all the juice from the pulp of Face Book Canvas to get the message of your new found passion in business on social media network to friends. Use the latest carousel format to exhibit photos, videos targeting Face Book's 89% followers as you keep in mind the business overall objective. You've a choice to use five photos with alternative links on Face Book Canvas.

- Narrate Your Company Story with Style.

A good story draws the audience to the speaker in the same way magnets attract metals. You're not sure of the opening line to grab audience attention. Use story opening. The duration of video clips allowed on Face Book Canvas is 2 minutes.

You can split up and use 15-20 second video clips spread out in the Canvas with complementary text messages.

Choose video clips that balance with text message. No matter the technique, creativity, purpose should be the number one priority for using visuals in social media as a marketing campaign strategy.

- Craft Clear Concise Calls to Action

Your ultimate aim is to move customers to take action in marketing. Make calls to action clear, concise, easy to understand with step by step instructions. You want subscribers to download the podcast, new clients to subscribe to the newsletter. Don't be vague. Show these on your Face Book Canvas Ad page.

- Pick on Visual Which evoke Emotion

Use a variety of visuals on Face Book Canvas to narrate the story of your company vision and mission. Photos, graphics, videos which add color to the buyer should take center stage on the Canvas. Solicit comments and testimonials from satisfied customers with tailor made videos to meet your company goals.

- Deliver on Promise with Audience Interest in Mind

Knowing your customers gives you a head start advantage over the competitor to create superior quality content that drive the message of the product/service home. Be aware of the effect of audience demographics in the message.

Sample this audio podcast interview transcript text from upcoming band.

- Music Makers

MUSIC INSERT: HEAVY METAL BEAT FADE UNDER IN 0:03 SECS. CROSS FADE TO APPLAUSE OF CHEERING CROWD

BAND LEADER (MALE): One day our band will be the biggest in the world

FEMALE VOCALIST ...And we shall be better than Boys 2 Men

PRESENTER: Now (PAUSE) that is success....

FADE IN MUSIC APPROX 0:05 SECS. FADE UNDER & MAINTAIN

SFX: LIQUID POURED INTO GLASS

FEMALE VOCALIST: We owe it all to Metro FM Radio Station

MALE BAND LEADER: Yeah! We threatened to burn down the studio if they don't play our CDs...

FEMALE VOCALIST: No. The studio gave us the next big thing. We got to play in front of key decision makers in the music industry and won 25 recording time contract at Ken wide Studios for our new album.

PRESENTER: What message do you have for your fans?

MALE BAND LEADER: Download more of our music from iTunes. We haven't changed a bit.

PRESENTER: To find out more about this band email ghettoband@ gmial.com, visit the website; follow them on Face Book, Twitter, Pinterest and Instagram.

Summary

Marketing is the heartbeat of doing online business. Making Social Media the cornerstone foundation of marketing strategy is the surest way of measuring development, growth and Return on Investment of your business. This chapter shows you Dozen Diverse Ways of Using Face Book, points out Four Trusted Marketing Tips and Techniques, and walks you through Six Simple Steps to Create Face Book Canvas Ads

Whether you use audio or add video podcast to the digital mix, the ultimate aim in podcast marketing strategy is to grow your business.

- Chapter 5 –

How to Maximize Podcast Marketing Strategy with Virtual Reality

You're passionate about using virtual reality on social media. What kind of images should you use? Where can you get ready to use free from copyright images online?

If you're looking for social media information, Social Media Marketing Podcast is the place to turn. Social Media Marketing Podcast shares information on podcasting marketing strategies from players in the industry on radio talk show. This radio talk show draws from top ten blogs written on the subject. Bloggers share unique tips and techniques on different aspects of podcasting as well as answer questions from listeners.

This chapter focuses on the role of virtual reality as a powerful podcast marketing strategy tool. Stay Focused on Outcome with Six Podcast Basics. Your individual participation has far reaching effect on the target audience. Get podcasting right with Five Personality Traits that Influence Successful Marketing Strategy Outcome by acquiring knowledge and skills on Ten Reasons Why You should add Video to the Digital Mix. Discussion on Five Effective Ways of Using Virtual Reality precedes Seven Sneaky Ways Virtual Reality Adds to Podcasting outlined in this chapter.

Stay Focused on Outcome with Six Podcast Basics

- Purpose Determines Content

Your goal is to increase business profit margin by 5% in three months of successful podcasting in order to triple income from $100-300. You aim to excite customers to download audio/video podcasts to generate this revenue. The purpose to create quality podcast content is doable with clear business set standards.

- Podcast Duration

You've chosen video/audio podcast to reach the target audience. Select suitable podcast duration. You're targeting senior citizens. The message and music in the podcast should favor target audience preference. Sounds of the sixties for music and half to forty five minute podcast duration are ideal for senior citizens with time to spare for listening and watching.

Use Power Point Presentation for online start up business entrepreneurs in video podcasting. Think of using colorful slides, video clips and graphs to show business lifecycle, facts and figure variations indicating trends.

Your want to create linkages with start up business for future deals. You also want visuals to emphasize details in the mind of customers to contact you for more information on the product/service.

- People Oriented Content

People love reading, hearing and watching success stories on videos. Quotations by authority figures on the subject add credence to the podcast. Name dropping of authority figures, celebrities, shakers and movers of business industry is a good way to produce people oriented content podcast.

Give adequate information on the topic of discussion. Remember doctor's rule of thumb. "Overdose is as bad as under dose." Customers have other obligations in life. Spare them information overload. When you've scripted the content, put it aside and take a look at it again with a fresh mind after sometimes. You weed out unwanted information, tweak and fine tune the final product in the episode by giving it time to simmer.

- Practical Level

Plan every stage of podcast set up, episode presentation with practical and easy to understand details. Keep practical life illustrations simple to emphasize main points of discussion. Use an outline to guide you through this process. The outline is your road map.

If you can't remember the name or function of equipment, that should not bother you. The equipment will work anyway and that is all you need to know.

- Pass the Message Effectively with Pictures – Internet Television

"The World has Gone Digital, so Should You." Look around in case you've not noticed. If you're yet to embrace virtual reality in podcasting, do it now!

Technology is running your life, home and business, whether you choose to ignore or acknowledge. Virtual reality is an idea that is here to stay. The best way to make the most of virtual reality in podcasting is to take control and use it to your advantage to market business and improve your lifestyle.

- Participate in Marketing Business with the Podcasting. Your Business Life Depends on It.

"Purpose determines content," is first mentioned in "Ways to Grab Audience Attention, "featured in chapter two. However, purpose is also the running theme throughout audio/video podcasting. It begins with engaging audio/video podcast audience by dangling benefits before their eyes. This is the added advantage of video podcast appeal. The viewer gets the message in living sound and sight. Purpose originates from the podcaster. This book opens with six qualities of a successful podcaster.

This chapter is not a revision of the qualities that set successful podcasters apart from the crowd in section one but revitalization of additional qualities that make your podcasting unique and user friendly. Here are five Personality Traits that influence the Outcome of Successful Marketing Strategy through podcasting.

Five Personality Traits Influence Podcast Marketing Strategy Outcome

Marketing is the process of identifying business potential opportunities to satisfy customer needs as well as increase business profit margin. You've a product/service idea. How will the audience know your product/service is in the market? You tell them.

Chapter one features seven qualities which set successful podcasters from the rest of the crowd. In this chapter, the focus is on institutional framework of podcasting as a marketing strategy. You're a brand. You're also part of the institution of your niche of interest in the business community. What additional leadership qualities do you need to ensure success in podcasting? Sample these five supplementary qualities of the model podcaster.

- Self confidence

You have a dream to fulfill in life. Everyone does. The dream could be obscured by childhood upbringing, culture, need to conform to society, but it can never be obliterated. You can turn that dream into reality by discovering your passion, singling out a vision and setting achievable goals based on self confidence.

If anyone tells you differently, the person could succeed in exciting you for a moment but true satisfaction comes from doing what you love with self confidence. You can't buy, borrow or bargain for self confidence any other way. You've got to have self confidence together with intelligence to run successful podcasting.

- Cognitive – Intelligence

You've 100% unique brain, so does everyone else. Most people only use 5% of brain power potential, according to scientific research discovery. 95% of valuable brain capacity is latent.

Tap into the latent 95% and use some of it to speak tenderly to the audience. Get them hyped up to buy. You can change lives and lifestyles through one podcast episode faster than you would with conferences on different physical locations around the globe. Use reasoning to strike a balance in podcast content presentation. Remember, customer's response maintains the life of your podcasting marketing strategy and is responsible for the business growth.

"Until thought is linked with purpose, there is no intelligent accomplishment," James Allen, psychologist of the human soul wrote.

- Be Open Minded

Old business tips and techniques that worked the year you were born are no longer sound. New exciting careers are created in different fields including your preferred niche.

Business opportunities abound with great potential for development; growth and expansion require innovative and creative ways to get the message of your product/service across to clients and customers effectively and efficiently.

The letter "O," in the word podcast stands for organization is used in the acronym in chapter three section one of this book. Think of organization as organized common sense.

- Patience Pays

Patience is a virtue that you cultivate over a period of time in business. You can't afford to be impatient with subscribers on the podcast. You lose customers when one or two discover a tinge of impatience in answering their questions. Don't lose vent your anger on subscribers.

- Energy

Passion + Purpose are exceptional qualities of a successful entrepreneur = Satisfaction. You podcast to fulfill purpose and you're driven by passion. Passion sets you apart from the rest of the crowd. The uniqueness of the five fingers on your hand illustrates unity in diversity of the fingers to work in harmony.

The words of Paul the apostle of Jesus Christ recorded in the New Testament book of Philippians 4:8, highlights the qualities of flourishing entrepreneur,

"Whatever things are true, whatever things are noble, whatever things are just, whatever things are pure, whatever things are lovely, whatever things are of good report, if there is any virtue and if there is anything praiseworthy — think on these things," Philippians 4:8. How do you know what is true and pure in video podcasting? Be guided by Top Ten Reasons Why You Should Add Video to the Digital Mix.

Top Ten Reasons Why You should add Video to the Digital Mix

Face Book video views rose from 4 to 8 billion in less than a year in 2015. In another development, mobile devices recorded an increase of 60% "watch time."

Video content is on the lead. Technology is turning passive consumers into active producers of content using basic equipment to run podcast. High end video equipment is highly recommended for better video quality. But in the absence and limitation of funds to acquire the expensive video gear, you get by with smart phone.

A good iPhone will give you quality video content if the phone is used well with overall objective of the business in mind. No matter the equipment, whether you use iPhone or special video equipment; the outcome is determined by taking ten tips thrown into the Digital Mix Marketing Strategy Promotion. Whether the video is used in email hacking to drive organic traffic, podcast, presentation the ultimate goal is to develop and improve business solutions.

- Understand Customer Needs

The significance of knowing the customer through research, customer care service, purchase power reveal areas of opportunity to tap into the core needs of potential clients and customers. Avoid drawbacks which stand defiantly on the way. These stumbling blocks prevent you from touching base and connecting with customers through different promotion avenues and awareness campaigns.

Emails, videos, websites, social media are avenues for promotion at your disposal. Choose the most effective to use in reaching the customers with the message.

- Underline the Place and Power of Video in Podcast

There is no one fit size for all podcasting method. When it comes to podcasting, there is no surer way of cutting costs, speeding the process of communication, improving reliability than creating superb content and throwing video clips for illustration into the mix.

Visuals show and drive the main point of the message home fast. Vary video clips with still photos for variety in the podcast. The choice of video stream, still photos, graphics is determined by among other things the type of target audience.

- Set Achievable Goals

Planning to set up and launch successful podcast talk about in chapter one include content creation. You know the audience. Next you need content and pass the message across to the target audience. You could choose video podcast for two reasons.

- Customer satisfaction – How will the video clips in the content challenge and change customers perception of your product/service?
- Call to Action – What action do you want customers to take towards the product/service? Get the customer to take action.
- Uncertainty Chats Pathway to Failure

Shooting and editing videos for promotion is not rocket science. You can use iPhone to take quality pictures. In this era of Do-It-Yourself you don't need special tutoring on video shooting. If you can read and understand instructions on equipment manual, you can work the smart phone to shoot video clip pictures and take still photos for promotion. All the information you need on video shooting, editing and publishing is available online.

Social media, email, apps are some of the most common channels of product/service promotion. Identify the platform to promote your product/service – You Tube, Face Book, Intagram, Snap Chat are outlet channels to consider using.

- Basic Equipment

The choice of equipment to use depends on your level of understanding of the market and channel of communication. You've been using smart phone. You might want to switch to higher grade professional equipment for better quality output. You have five basic set of equipment to run podcast show, should professional equipment be prohibitive. Here is the basic set of equipment to run on.

- Digital Video Camera – Takes still photos and videos.

- Tripod – Shaky pictures reflect shaky foundation.

- Microphone – Whether you're doing audio/video podcast, a good dynamic microphone is a must have.

- Cue lights to brighten the background for crisp pictures.

- Studio – A room in your house would do fine.

- Unravel Stand Alone Pitfall on the Show.

Share the platform with talents. Experts in the industry, guests, provide great video interview clips in podcast episodes. You shouldn't hog all the limelight. Think of producing the show by putting in all the right ingredients to get required outcome.

- Shape Up or Ship Out

What are the competitors doing? Read, watch, listen, compare and contrast notes with professionals in your niche. What customer service approach works well? Learn as much as you can to stay on top of the game by shaping up your podcast. If you don't shipping out is starring you on the face.

- Platform

You have a choice between self or shared hosting. These two have advantages and disadvantages. Select the platform with the greatest following to use. You Tube has a huge fan base, tap into the wider market opportunity on this channel. Your website is another avenue. Snap chat, Periscope, Vine are open avenues for promotion.

- Video Connection

Video posted on YouTube…. should have links leading to your website. Including links on the video to direct viewers to your landing page on the site. Aim for 3000 downloads and you're in business online with a big bang.

- Ultimate podcast Price

Use feedback from downloads, clicks to show sales promotion progress and podcast progress performance. Call ins, increase of traffic are other indicators that show podcast is on course. Upgrade to premium standard when necessary.

Business prosperity is measured in a variety of ways. Don't limit your measuring yardstick to the few most common methods. If the podcast is not yielding expected results consider scaling up to make the most of social media visuals in monetizing podcast.

Five Effective Methods of Using Virtual Reality in Podcasting Marketing Strategy

Potential of virtual reality is used in different industries to promote business development and growth. Here are five common areas.

- Virtual Tours

Cruise Liners, Colleges, Camp Organizers, special interest destinations make mileage with video podcast to market tour destinations.

Architects, graphic artists' impressions of model creations reflect reality of the place, person or part of equipment envisioned. These model creations provide viewers with advance first hand opportunity to view the finished product up close and candid.

- Training for Tomorrow

Hands on training assist apprentices to learn fast. This experience is used in real life situations. Picture an apprentice physiotherapist training on a real patient with physical disability. The result could be a recipe for disaster. That is the reason for sitting long hours to study human body part functions and watching video clips in med school to know how these parts function under normal circumstances is all about.

- Event Organizers

The 1985 live coverage of Ethiopian famine relief had great effect on the audience. Viewers in developed countries gave towards this worthy cause having watched the live show performance by top cream musicians singing "We are the World," in support of the event which was relayed by telecast to millions of viewers around the world.

You can get into this number of viewers for your product/service with podcast and it wouldn't cost much as the live band aid of 1985.

- Show Case Products

Economic based factors contribute to Soap Operas popularity as well as showcase products. Video clip adverts ranging from domestic products, cosmetics to toiletry; provide variety targeting the female viewer.

Mini problems are solved through these advertisements. A woman is satisfied when hover cleans up the mess; the husband's shirt is cleaned in a matter of seconds by the detergent. Advertisers achieve great success with video clip promotion of products. You can do the same with Face Book Canvas for Works.

- Communication Has Gone Hi-tech

Visuals play two main roles in television news coverage. You can see it as it happens. 'This is the BBC News' demonstrated both in graphics, spoken words and vision. The caption and image of the world rotating on it axis is the latest scientific approach to presenting the news to viewers around the world.

This approach suggests a realistic coverage of events, rid of bias before the viewer's own eyes. Visual narrative in television is significant in documentation of events while spoken narrative contributes information. Why use visuals in social media? You can borrow a whole load of techniques from television programming to use in video podcasting. The outcome is better marketing strategy for the product/service to monetize your podcast. That is the reason why you should add video to your digital mix. Virtual Reality Adds Color and Vitality to Podcasting.

Seven Significant Ways Virtual Reality Adds Liveliness to Podcasting

- Grab Target Audience Attention.

Viewers are spoilt for choice by television programs. Television stations are outdoing one another with improved ground-breaking ways to attract viewers to shows in a variety of ways. The audiences you're targeting get quality content from adverts with images from television shows to compare and contrast with your podcast.

If your virtual reality quality is below international standards, you stand to lose the audience to favorite television programs. Securing and maintaining audience attention requires using podcast with images which demand viewers' attention. Social media visuals account for 44% of all social media activity.

Video podcasting fire is fast catching up with online contests popularity. 80% of online video streams originate from Face Book, statistics in Social Media Marketing Podcast reveal. Not to mention emerging Face Book Live Video. How long would it take you to watch 110 years of video footage in store? A lot of video clips in stock are directly fed into Face Book.

This mammoth volume of video footage indicates the potential video has in podcasting content creation. Visual contents rank number 3 in hierarchy of importance and use. Increasing impressive statistic figures sound great but it requires hard work to achieve. Here are seven different ways visuals are used to brand product message, customer care, all wrapped up in content. Ignore these seven ways at the peril of your business.

Whether you're an old hand at using social media or starting out, the basic principles and steps of using visuals are the same. Phew! That is a relief.

- Selection of Social Media Visuals.

What type of visuals best suit your podcast audience? Is your system compatible with the format of the visuals?

If you're running on XP you're aware of limitations this software has in playing back videos from different sources. You could get by with YouTube but not all of the other channels hence the message "We are sorry your system does not support...."

Here are expert ideas on what you should look for in social media outlet channel to run successful podcasting.

- Landing Page

How interactive is your landing page? 3 things make up a good landing page.

- Information

- Blog Content

- Free Downloads

The above three elements are discussed in different sections of this book in details. Take note of them.

- Types of Visuals

Images double up as content with text headers, followed by description. Be creative. Let your juice flow. Get customers glued to their seats as you deliver milestone podcast episodes to market your product/service. Make time. Play back excerpt of podcast episode in the presence of your spouse without soliciting comment. If your spouse stops to watch and comment, you've a winner. You get the same reaction from potential clients and customers.

If the spouse is not moved, you've more work to blend images with text in your podcast to influence the audience's decision. Get back to basics. Remember to plan every detail of the podcast episode including images you intend to use.

- Individual Designs

You've a rough idea of the audience reaction to the message from research. Use this information as a benchmark to select the kind of images that appeal to the audience. Take into consideration age. In the process of selection, create categories of images in order of ranking individual designs.

Share quotes, tips, photos on the podcast to spice up the presentation. There are tons of free materials online without restriction you can use. Go to Gipsy for samples.

Another category of visuals to look into is "must do activities," in this exercise. Get the items in your check list, tutorials, images, whatever draws the audience to make informed choices about the product/service you're promoting based on quality content creation ready to go with to do list check off system.

Third, category includes graphics, video clips, slides and live video streams. Spend time scouring the reefs for these "show pieces," especially, if you're using images created by others. Select the best, leave out the rest.

Articles with running text commentaries address specific problems in life. These articles take the reader/viewer through simple steps to solve challenges through sight and sound. Shop around in Skitch, Snagit for sample images to use in your social media outreach campaign strategy.

- Mobile Tools.

You've readymade Canvas for Works to change the features of chosen visuals to suit the audience flavor. This feature has the facility to upload, organize and resize images. Check it out in advance to get a feel of individual design images for social media use. These two together with others in the market have down to earth easy to read and understand instructions anyone keen on podcasting can use with great success.

- Mobile Tools

Technology is shrinking devices to small sizes for easy handling and transportation, yet maintains high quality performance. Who would have known the original huge computer unit would come down to a laptop or phone booths would be replaced by hand held mobile phones.

You want to add images with text in social media. No problem. Over and Phonto are designed to give you back value for money. In return you get iOs Android apps used in telephone communication with smart phones to tap into online available resources at your disposal.

WordSwag and Typorame also offer designs that assist to overlay text with images. These two only provide iOS.

If you're keen on exploring other available avenues, studios and Brandr are the latest developments with fabulous features that work across different social media platforms to create images for sharing with your peeps. Get all you need to make visual reality significant part of your social media marketing campaign. Whatever your need, there is a product in store for it.

Summary

This chapter forms the basic framework of video podcasting. You learn to Stay Focused on Outcome with Six Podcast Basics and Five Personality Traits that influence individual marketing strategy success outcome when you apply Top Ten Reasons Why You Should Add Virtual reality to the Digital Mix. In the process, you get Five Effective Methods of Marketing podcasting going to achieve Seven Significant Ways Virtual Reality Adds Liveliness to your podcast.

– Chapter 6 -

How to Monetize Your Podcast

You fancy modern technology and warm up to the change and challenge of careful adjustment to your appearance before the presentation. You adjust the toupee, smirk at the camera, coming on strong with "Live from Texas, it is the Oil Mining USA Ltd. Sign off with, "This is Mike G. Oil Company Secretary, Texas returning you to our head office. The zoom lens gives SCOPE. "We'll just go over to your memo of July 4th," you pronounce as slides of the chairman's portrait and weather charts in the distant branches fill in any gaps in the program.

Three decades ago, such modern technology advances were remotely conceivable. Communication has been enlivened, not just by telephone conference system that anyone could use, simply by asking the GPO to connect you to as many as seven separate phones at once and paying only as much as if all the calls had been made separately. Internet connectivity has ushered in new ways of doing business and effective means of communication patterns in the advent of information age.

It's not enough to set up and launch audio/video podcasting. You must also know the impact of the advertisement, which in the past, sales persons performed at a conferences in one city, a lecture in another and a product demonstration in the next, all on the same date. That is all in the past.

You're now secure in the knowledge that audio/video podcasting recordings leave you free for the important business, which is lunch with potential clients at the club. It has to do with the company blog, although heaven knows it could be bland presentation of the product you're selling.

The traditional company report is at stake. The presentation of company accounts should spell things out, as most shareholders and employers are not trained financial experts. A financial expert finds nothing wrong "seeing turnover is $90m and the trading profit is $5m, but to the non expert it looks ridiculous."

"Five Priceless Qualities of Perfect Podcast," in chapter one touched on listeners' questions and answers. The assumption is that you have all the answers to business finance challenges and problems. Most subscribers are not financial experts. But experts know that all the usual items, such as cost of materials, wages and services are deducted from gross income to get the profit margin.

What company reports need is diagrams, such as pictures of mugs with liquid labeled "turnover," with different levels signifying money gone in dividends or paying for the attendant to change roller towels. It is counterproductive to use images like cakes split into profits and wages. Subscribers are at a loss wondering why the knife couldn't be shifted to give employee pay a larger slice.

Scientific discovery suggests that between a third and half of all civil service meetings would be done ear to ear rather than person to person. Another quarter could be done satisfactorily over television but it goes on to warn that taking the process too far might "increase the volume of communication more than is considered desirable."

In a lay person's language, there comes a point in which you have to stop gabbing and get on with the task at hand. And the task of this chapter is to answer the question "How do you monetize podcasting against the background of obstacles starring you in the face?" You'll learn "How to Monetize Your Podcast," with Five Impacts of Social Media which Tip Earning in Your Favor, become aware of Six Signs that show Your Podcast is on Course by embracing Six Essential Elements for Monetizing Podcast.

"Video Podcast is demandingly challenging, but the pay back is very high with generous fringe benefits, and, of course should you fail, there is always the haven, no one will get hurt but you."

5 Impacts of Social Media Tip Earning in Your Favor

How do you gauge the impact of social media on business development and growth? Social media is to online small business, what physical nourishment is to the human body. You can't have one without the other. These two co-exist to meet needs from both ends of the spectrum to grow business and keep the body healthy respectively.

73% of small business owners use social media to improve business, latest survey by Clutch reveals. What favorite social media outlets are popular with small business owners?

If you're not using social media, you're missing out on the real deal of doing business online. 89% online companies are already using Face Book to reach out and connect with customers and potential clients. Twitter is in the second position with popularity rating of 49% followed by LinkedIn at 42% and Pinterest gaining grounds with 31%. These social media outlets are on the upper end of popularity scale.

On the lower end of social media scale are Snapchat 11%, Vine 8% and Periscope with 4%. These are not numbers merely floated to boost social media popularity. Social media does work. These numbers reflect the impact of social media in growing online small businesses. All the small businesses using social media must be doing something right for the business to keep on using these channels of communication.

Websites trail social media in popularity with 65% according to Clutch survey. Your aim in using social media goes beyond the hype for "likes," to forecasts and sales of product/service promotion. How do you select the right social media to expand your small business?

Clutch survey credited with above social media findings has done the hard work to outline five easy to read and understand ways you can use to tap into social media in growing your small business online.

- Increase Business Income

The emphasis throughout this book is on discovering the unique selling point to market your product/service. Your overall objective in doing business is to monetize podcast to increase income in the business. The exercises used to achieve this goal shape the framework of doing business with a difference.

- Images and Text Formats

"A picture is more than a thousand words," is not just a cliché. You depend on sight to sample the surrounding landscape. You believe what you see. Images speak volumes in video podcasting.

If your audience survey tips the balance of content to images, Instagram or Pinterest are the two choices famed for image communication. LinkedIn is a better choice for audiences that prefer reading long articles. You do well to mix and match images and text for maximum effect.

- Identify the Best time for Posting.

What good does it do the business to post on social media unless you target a specific audience with the message? You need to read the signs of the times. Understand the target audience preference and engagement with social media platform to get the most out of using this channel of communication to reach out and touch the needs of your target audience with product/service content.

You should time posting content on social media to coincide with the presence of the greatest number of target audience online. You'll be amazed how effective social media is to your listening and viewing audiences if you post messages on prime time. You know your audience. You also need know the time of great activity of the audience on social media.

- Insightful Business Niche

You're looking for good reviews for your business to market the services to potential clients in the hospitality industry. Yelp is the social media channel to use. Using this social media outlet will rank your eatery business high among consumers.

Hospitality industry has fantastic mouth watering dishes you always wanted to try out. If you run a small restaurant and is keen to attract hungry folks to the venue, online provides you with social media platform fit for your business needs as long as you've insight into the business niche to craft get the right content out to the right audience.

- Indicators of Business Progress

Use social media survey figures to steer you in the right direction to choose the right kind of social media outlet for your business audience. Whatever you do for the business in social media, to identify peak hours of audience activity, choosing images over text, insight into the business niche, verifying business progress should be in line with the overall objective of your business. How disappointed your audience must be if you do not deliver on promise.

Podcast is the obvious step forward in broadcasting, recording and communication. The vast majority of new equipment pouring into the market daily is made to meet your every need for quality sound/video podcasting. The equipment is half the weight, half the size and is backed by years of proven record of reliability to deliver on promise.

You've the equipment. Get the message out now and touch someone's life with podcast content to increase sales. Which indicators tip podcast earning in your favor?

Five Silent Signs Your Podcast Is on Course.

- Priority

Hosea's retirement age worked him out of the lucrative locomotive engine train driver job. First he got lump sum amount of money to set up house before getting accrued benefits and gratuity of over five decades of dedicated service to the corporation. He bought land in prime agricultural area and put up a spacious house for the family.

Five years down the line, money ran out including subsidies from commercial crop plantation income. Tough times came tumbling in. Squabbles and misunderstanding erupted in the once close nit family unit.

Hosea woke up at six one Monday morning having spent a sleepless night deliberating on the way forward. He bolted to the farm leaving instructions behind,

"Wake up and follow me to the garden." Hosea's family members understood and knew from the tone of his voice he meant every word. The wife and children followed shortly and found him swinging the hoe as if he was mad with the soil.

In five short months of hard work, the family harvested grain for the first time in years, had the kitchen garden supplying vegetables, onions and tomatoes and the petty squabbles disintegrated into the background. What made the difference? Hosea put his priority into perspective.

If you want the business to grow, change your thinking and your priority will change as well. The activities you undertake to grow the business, podcast included are pieces of the jigsaw puzzle on your Return On Investment picture.

- Marketing

You've a product/service that would earn you profit. No customer will purchase items kept under key and lock in the warehouse. If you want millions to know about your product/service in the shortest time possible, resort to use online marketing strategy this book talks about.

These approaches to online business are fast, efficient and cost effective. Have you ever considered starting an online store for your product to step up sales? You've more flexibility to manage online store compared to brick and mortar establishment. You communicate directly to the client who would place the order and in no time pay the money into your account in exchange for goods delivered. You save time, money and energy doing business online. You think online marketing strategy is hearsay. Try it out

- Resource Management

You're passionate about doing business online. You've a product/service ready but unsure how to go about podcasting. Solicit assistance of a friend. You could also team up with someone in the industry who knows which strings to pull in making sales online.

In three months of operation, your business should show signs of growth. In one year you could set up brick and mortar establishment shop as contact point to distribute products for local consumption. Your online success story goes to prove the point that good resource management is part of doing booming business.

- Incentives – Give Away

You're unable to self publish due to financial constraints as a writer. You've no one to blame if the book manuscript you labored to write for years never gets published. The opportunity to market your book online for free through giving away a course on writing is your ticket to get published. Take the liberty to mention your work on the podcast as well as give away writing incentives.

This is the "big picture," thinking way of doing business. No one will know you wrote a book manuscript on an important subject if you don't get the word out there. Podcast presents the greatest appeal to reach a wide audience online. "Where there is a will, there is a way," you've and know, Do-It-Yourself.

It's hard to discuss a company's products without mentioning incentives. You read about giving away incentives to attract clients and sell more in chapter one. Are still with us? Great!

Think of incentives in terms of investing in the customer. You get out what you put into the business, hence the acronym "GIGO," Garbage In, Garbage Out used for illustration at the beginning of this book. You have tons of stuff to give away for free in exchange for enormous business returns.

Another way of growing your home based online writing business is through blogging. You get noticed and with time establish your credibility as author to sell your books online. Why not use multiple channels to cease the opportunity now and watch your business grow to a vast online business empire in future. Steve Jobs, Bill Gates, started where you're. Today, these gentlemen are house hold names. What did they do differently? How did they do it? The circumstances could be different; the passion unique to individual but the opportunity is available for you as it was for them.

- Flexibility

If you're skeptical of doing things differently your business growth is stunted. You're in the hospitality industry selling fast foods down town. A number of customers have asked for fruit salad. You don't do fruits.

How about setting up and running podcast on take away fruit salad? You could double the income with home delivery of your favorite gourmet and fruit salad give away incentive. There is no reason your fast food business can't offer specialized food service delivery if you're flexible to listen with understanding to customer requests.

Six Essential Elements for Monetizing Podcast

Monetizing podcast require that you distinguish product/service to meet specific audience need in order to stimulate purchase. Six essential elements stand out in the marketing mix to assist with monetizing podcast. Place promotion on top of your priority list of the marketing mix.

- Product/Service

Identify a product/service which meets customer need in a particular area of life. Personal, professional, family, finance, health and fitness are specific areas of human needs your product aims to address. Position your product in the market and compete with other professionals on an equal playing field in quality, class and price once you identify the right product/service for the right audience.

If you're in the transport industry with a fleet of vehicles covering a variety of streets for hire in a large suburban area. How do you know where each vehicle is at any given time? You can call to confirm. Eventualities can foul up instant telephone communication at any time. Install an automatic monitoring system to keep tabs on all errant vehicles and public conveyance.

Miniature low powered transmitters placed at signposts at intersections and selected points would transmit a unique code which identifies that specific point. When integrated by radio from control center, the vehicle's receiver automatically sends back the stored code number. The computer at the center remembers these facts and can locate any selected vehicle to within several hundred feet of its true position on any signpost street.

Do you see the business opportunity for car manufacturers in this? What if you secured the contract to act as the intermediary between the plant making this device and transport vehicle owners? In the book "17 Principles of Success," Napoleon Hill sums up this point beautifully with the following quote,

"Opportunity is everywhere, but it is fleet of foot. Even if you have the vision to recognize it, without a fast decision on your part, it will be gone." The book is edited by Mathew Sartwell.

- Pricing Policy

Price refers to the value you attach to the product/service. Pricing policy also signify the value customers attach to the product/service. Pick on the right price for the right product with the right audience in mind.

- Place – Outlet for goods/service.

In brick and mortar establishment business, a warehouse is ideal for storage of goods. Goods are sold by retailers in shops and supermarkets. In the hospitality industry, services are confined to restaurants. Online business has no boundary, no geographical location and no bottle necks. The world is your market. You couldn't meet the need of everyone shuttling back and forth online. That is why you identify target group and tailor your content to meet their specific needs. In return, you get customers to buy product/service if you monetize podcasting.

- Promotion and Provision

In relation to product development and marketing,

- You promote development of new methods of reaching customers with the message. This exercise exposes entrepreneurs and new products to the target audiences as well as creates quality awareness of the product/service in the market.

- Identify and test alternative marketing channels. Adapt appropriate methods to enhance business success to meet the demand. What do you want to say about your product that is unique? You may want to inform, persuade, or remind the target audience of the benefits of your product. Whatever method you choose, should be geared towards yielding tangible measurable results. Chapter four deals with marketing strategy.

Reaching Out to Retirees

You want to create content encouraging young people to consider saving up for retirement. Your target group is approximately 19-45 years of age. What message do you have for this age group?

You aim is to convince this group to save 10% income per annum on fixed account, 45% on operating costs, food, running the car, paying tuition and emergency medical expenses. 25% should be designated to investment, down payment on a house, 15% on clothes, buying a new car, and households. The remaining 5% should be set aside for miscellaneous use. These are the facts you must convert to convince the audience in the content.

- Price Winning Awards.

Competition is an effective tool for promotion. The process reflects and generates ideas for new product/service. Multimillion companies such as Coca Cola spend a fortune on competitions and advertising.

- Training

If you're in the publishing industry, offer free special training courses on your blog to customers in that category. Lead customers to your blog and website to get more information and make orders.

- Action Oriented Research

The market is flooded with new products/services. You want yours to stand out, engage in action oriented research to curve a niche for your product/service.

- People - Target Audience

Online business allows you to have access to a wide selection of the market and promises a great potential audience. Audience research is vital in knowing the target audience and how best to reach them with information. Decide whether to use audio/video podcasting to promote the business.

- Process

What steps do customers take to access your product/service? Time taken in this exercise constitute process. If you invite subscribers to visit your website for more information on the product/service, be sure the website is easily navigable.

It is all very well to have high end tech website but if switching from landing page to online form the customer needs to fill for membership presents hustle, the process is plagued with technical hurdle.

WordPress has one of the simplest links. Customers can comment, offer suggestions for improvement and access additional information from your site easily with WorPress. Keep it simple. Here are six simple steps to adopt in developing effective communication strategy.

- Discover Target Audience

Identifying the customer is the first step in the process of marketing strategy. All other details of podcasting come second.

- Determine Overall Objective of Communication

Customers are hard pressed for time and patience to cope with pressure in other areas of life. Select the format with most appeals to the audience. You've set up audio podcast for customers. Make it exciting by using fitting illustrations to "drive the nail on the head," as they say.

- Design Message to meet Customer need

Flaunt benefits of the product/service in the content.

- Decide on Promo mix

Use a variety in the promotional mix to attract and drag the audience through to a satisfying close in the episode.

- Settle on the medium of communication - audio/video
- Gather feedback

"A word rashly spoken cannot be brought back even by a chariot or four horses," a Chinese proverb says.

Human beings are endowed with verbal and non verbal effective ways of communication. Words for example are windows used for guiding, instructing and warning. Yet words can be misinterpreted.

You get feedback, comments from subscribers, producers, consumers, forums and special groups. Businesses bend over backwards to promote product/service. If you block feedback in one or all of the following four ways, the end result of the exercise is a recipe for disaster.

- Allowing no questions even though you asked the audience to contribute by asking questions.

- Addressing the audience and not having eye contact on camera during video podcasting recording.

- Asking ambitious questions during audience, market research and podcasting.

You can improve podcasting with a number of actions from feedback to monetize this exercise.

- Email

Social network is a great way to get feedback from subscribers on face book, Pinterest and Twitter among others.

- Call In Program

Instant feedback provides liveliness to connect with the audience and presence in the podcast.

- Research – Research is an ongoing exercise in business. Research the audience, market, product to improve your serve in all stages of the business lifecycle.

- Disquss

Technology is breaking down the digital barrier giving producers and consumers equal opportunity to deliver on promise. If you've a lively audience following your blog, you get a stream of comments and suggestions on Disquss. Try it out. It works well both ways for you and the audience.

- Price Awards

Online businesses are running contests all the time. Whether money booker is offering a ticket to Rio Olympic 2016, Wimbledon music concert or voucher gifts in exchange for services, it boils down to price awards. Your business competitor is getting more visits online by running writing contest. Why not you?

Examine customers' response and use feedback and your unique selling point to drive the overall business objective home with catchy and promising phrase such as "Working with you today to build a better tomorrow."

Summary

Making money online is big business. Loads of cash exchange hands from business to business, business to individual and from individuals to business even as you read this now.

This chapter points out Five Impacts of Social Media, Six Signs your Podcast is Course and concludes with Six Essential Elements for Monetizing your Podcast. Justification - Time is not only money; it has a price tag on it.

- Chapter 7 -

How Podcast can Transforms Small Businesses to Vast Online Empires

Non Stop Video started out as a consultancy service in 1995. Music CDs were introduced to the market in Kenya around that time. Video tapes were in vogue for music and movies entertainment. The prospect of turning the video library business around from making loss to profit provided the opportunity of setting up and running video coverage service alongside managing the ailing video shop. This required

- Management and supervision of the video library with 1,000 members

- Improved Business Marketing Strategy and Development plan for service delivery

- Monitoring and evaluation of sales

In six months, this underperforming video library broke even and in three years, Non Stop Video realized turnover revenue to the tune of half a million US dollars, employees number increased from one to five full time and 3 part time subordinate staff members. The consultant mandated with this task recommended and the owner sold the business off at huge profit.

The potential for video coverage services to shoot weddings, funerals, computer class tutorials on video was a new direction the consultant could seize to tap into the new emerging market. This undertaking would open doors of opportunity online to shoot documentaries and expand in that field.

Today, podcasting would promote and take this business to the next level. Technology to expand the business is here. The market is bigger and better. The demand is ever increasing. How would you transform your Small Business into Vast Online Business Empire? This chapter unveils Podcasting as New Phase of Modern Method of Business marketing strategy. Stay ahead of the game with Ten Smart Ways to Make Podcast Profitable through Face Book Instant Articles.

Podcasting: New Phase of Modern Business

"Nothing is as powerful as an idea whose time has come," Victor Hugo the playwright wrote. Podcast is trending, timely and spot on marketing strategy in the business world today. However, not everyone reaps all the potential financial benefits from this exercise. If you're passionate about podcasting, nothing or no one can stop you. How do you monetize podcast to transform small business into online vast business empire?

There are as many unique ideas to grow business through podcasting. This chapter brings together time tested and true expert ideas business entrepreneurs can't do without.

Everything you need to know from understanding how to utilize, organize podcast content for profitability is available and easily accessible online. Whether you're starting out or need hints and tips to improve your business, podcast is the answer.

Six reasons stand out in using podcast to transform small business. The reasons include but not exclusive to investment, inspiration, market identity, introduction of product/service, incubation period and infrastructure. The "I," constant in these reasons trace significance of podcasting to the individual outlined in section one, chapter one and in chapter four.

- Investment

Financial institutions are slow in supporting start up business ventures. That is the bad news. On the bright side of life, new businesses pop up in the market by the thousands all the time. Not all new businesses stand the test of time to generate sufficient income to stay afloat in the industry.

Start up business failures amount to 80% annually, economic experts survey indicate. Majority of start ups are in the small business category. Insufficient capital investment, inadequate knowledge of market needs and lack of entrepreneurship skills are three main causes of high rate of start up business flops. Not many new business owners use podcast as a lucrative marketing strategy tool to grow the business.

Get smart. Think out of the box. Break the stalemate imposed by financial institutions to market your own business through podcasting. Do-it-Yourself (DIY) is the spirit of online business age. You should have no trouble with inspiration.

- Inspiration

"…don't give up trying to do what you really want to do. Where there is love and inspiration…you can't go wrong," Ella Fitzgerald said.

Online business cuts across all cultures. Your small business target audience is online. You hardly meet let alone see eye to eye with the audience, but you interact with every last one who visits your website for pleasure or business. You need inspiration to draw new clients and maintain old ones to the website. Take action. Get to work. Set up, launch podcast that suits your business goals and meets the audience psychological and physical needs today.

You've a product/service to offer. Podcast gives your businesses identity, platform, to market and sell your product/service cheaply and conveniently to clients through smart phone, tablet, and personal computer provided you identify the market.

- Identify the Market

You need to know about potential competitors of the same product/service in the market. Perform two kinds of research, primary and secondary at your disposal. Secondary research involves gathering published information from industry, journals, newspapers and magazines. Your primary research material is from online data base.

You can't exhaust internet material anymore than you can exhaust the potential of using your website to run successful small business. The Internet,

"It's like the world's biggest library - except all the books are on the floor," Frank Bass wrote in "The Associated Press: Guide to Internet Research and Reporting." Read reviews in your preferred field of business.

You need strategic marketing plan to podcast. Get statistics, numbers and sources to streamline the small business. Marketing plan forms the basis of your small business sales projection. No matter how brilliant your idea of small business is, marketing is mandatory. Marketing begins long before the business begins and continues long after sales projections trickle in. The secret is to maintain flow, to uncover hidden details, stay relevant in the market, once you introduce the product/ service to consumers online.

- Introduce Product/Service to Consumers

Nothing beats product/service advertisement online. Small, medium and large businesses are introduced into the market at one point. You've upgraded your website domain and paid for self hosting. You've unlimited opportunity to advertise direct or indirectly in addition to running podcast.

"To advance our careers, we're expected to promote ourselves unabashedly," Susan Cain writes in her book, "Quiet: The Power of Introverts in a World That Can't Stop Talking." You don't have the gift of gab. Don't let that deficit stand in the way of podcasting. You've the tools and techniques to change all that today. It might take a while before your sales pick up to start reaping benefits from the fruits of podcasting. Understand that the business has to pass through incubation period.

- Incubation Period

Think of incubation period as a time for nurturing small business to maturity from planning, setting it up, getting the business off the ground, and marketing to effectively running it. These four stages take time. But the value of incubation exceeds the waiting period in payback deals. All businesses start off small and grow to maturity. Your small business is no exception.

- Infrastructure

You don't have to be techno savvy to set up and run weekly successful podcast. Free lessons to get you up and running in no time are only a click of the mouse away online. If you're in doubt and need on spot check confirmation on any of this free information, trail off to FAQs section of any website.

Podcast really work. It's simple and straightforward to set up and get the business up and running. Put your business into perspective with Ten Smart Ways to Make Podcast Profitable today!

Ten Smart Ways to Make Podcast Profitable

1. Site Membership

Don McAllister, the brain behind <u>Screencasts Online</u> credits the popularity of site membership to his podcast traffic ranging in "several thousands." Don traces the success of his site membership to promotion in <u>Podcast Prodigy</u> during an interview.

2. Sell Support Team

It doesn't matter how good a player you're in volley or basketball team. Your brilliant performance does not guarantee lifting the trophy at the blow of the last whistle in the game. This is true of competitive sports as it is in business. Business is not stand alone exercise such as lifting weights in the gym. You need other players in the industry to make it big in business.

The player who serves volley ball does not also always spike at the net. That does not mean the player is stagnant on one position. During the game, players rotate, take turns to serve and spike. All six volley team members are good in different positions during play time and the team is credited with the win, not a single volley ball player.

In the publishing industry, a book manuscript idea originates from the author. Your manuscript is not complete without the graphic designer for the book cover. You also need a publisher for the finished product in print. Not to mention the agent to speed up the process. All the people involved in publishing your book are members of the same team playing in different positions.

You've worked hard to attract 3,000 downloads per podcast episode. Imagine charging for space in the episode. The sponsors have captive potential audience. You stand to benefit by selling space to sponsors with this figure of followers not just to one, not two, you could sell space to three sponsors depending on the duration of the advertisement and podcast episode.

3. Stand out in the Crowd

You want to initiate a relationship with potential clients. You'll never regret using podcasting. You build a huge fan base with podcast to buy your books in the publishing industry if that is your niche.

- Listen and Learn

What are other podcasters doing right to make it big in the industry? You can borrow a leaf or model them in your area of interest. Learn by listening to audio podcasts and watch a variety of video podcasts to get the feeling and understand what others have done in podcasts. In addition, use your ingenuity to create tailor made podcast content targeting your audience. Include, interviews, views, news, to stay relevant and within the framework?

Start discussion groups by sending out questions you plan to tackle on the coming episode in advance through email along with invites for guidance and direction to your subscribers.

- Theme Song – Signature tune is the identity of the radio broadcasting program. Use similar technique in podcasting. Music adds flavor to the podcast and reflects your professional touch while giving the show energy. Slot in music at the beginning, middle and end to act as stage upon which your voice stands in the podcast.

- Podcast Persona - Your character is the sum total of your thoughts.

- Be Passionate

- Be Real – Set realistic goals for the podcast. If you choose one podcast a week, deliver on promise. Your choice of the number of podcasts depends on your ability and outcome expectation.

- Be flexible. Stay focused. Make podcast interesting to listen and watch. Use humor in moderation. Whatever you do, keep the goal to increase downloads of your podcasts in mind.

How does making between $80-100k a month on books sound to you? Don't just dream about it; make it happen with podcast starting now. If you think this sounds too good to be true? Put podcast to the test then sit back and watch sales of your books swell. You're looking at six figures in a year writing online and podcasting to promote the services.

4. Seek Coaching Opportunities

Pick up any print magazine from newspaper vendor. You won't miss expert column on marriage, life, finance, health and fitness and the list is as long as human needs. Visit any online website and you get tons of coaching in writing, weight loss, anti aging and retirement among others.

Your expertise in one field of study is a gold mine in podcasting to help one, two three, 100 subscribers unlock doors of opportunity in different fields of interest. Podcast opens doors of opportunity for subscribers to seek better business opportunities and improve their lifestyle.

No one knows this better than Michelle Evans of the <u>Breaking Free podcast</u> fame. In the first year of launching her podcast, she has received between 7 to 15 emails from people requesting to hire her. Over half of the numbers of people interested in hiring you are potential future subscribers to your podcast. Whether coaching is free or paid, points out the need for individual self improvement. Cease the opportunity available to make mileage with podcasting today.

5. Selling Services

Mitch started out as small time IT engineer specializing in software installation. He soon discovered big opportunities in website development and couldn't resist the temptation to try his hands on new areas. His effort paid off over and above his wildest dreams.

Mitch set up and launched Pal Partnership in the process of expansion. This outfit boasts of an average of 3,500 listeners. Mitch has developed web sites for many of his listeners who request and are willing to pay well for his web development services.

6. Survey the Audience

Audience survey gives you information on quality and performance of product/service you're podcasting on. Chapter four emphasizes the role and importance of feedback. Audience survey is quick and preferable if you want information to improve on existing product/service.

You get to know the audience interest, become more aware of the product/service quality and able to deliver on promise.

7. Sign Up Rewards

You don't have to go for broke to sell products as an associate affiliate. Sandra started selling small stock of women cosmetics from her house in Perth, Western Australia on commission. In three years she had enough orders from saloons to warrant opening shop in the central business district of Perth.

Sandra got the cosmetics in bulk at wholesale price and sold single items at little lower than the market retail price. In three years, she had bought her dream car put down payment on a four bedroom house in up market section of Perth Metro area and was able to plan the lifetime abroad holiday dream. How did she get into the cosmetics business?

Cindy her high school girlfriend talked her into it. Sandra signed up as Cindy's friend to get the goods on credit on the strength of Cindy's reputation and good word. Cindy got her sign up reward for bringing Sandra aboard and Sandra discovered her passion to work in the cosmetic industry and make money.

8. Sell Subordinate Products

Human interest comes full circle in podcasting as an avenue for attracting and maintaining listeners/viewers interest. The interviewee stands a chance to talk about the product and the price.

Here is an excellent opportunity for the expert interviewee to offer discount on product/service with your associate code to the audience at the end of the interview. This is win-win situation for you and the guest speaker on your audio/video podcast.

9. Supplement Your Earning with e-Book from Podcast Materials

You've been podcasting for five, seven, ten years. You've accumulated a fare amount of podcast material as well as built solid clientele base to the tune of 6,000 subscribers and the number is on the increase. Your podcast download is over the 3,000 threshold to make podcast's special list. How about turn the material into e-book? It is doable and profitable.

Nick Loper did turn 500+ John Dee Duma's previous episodes "Entrepreneur on Fire," into e-book. Nick put together the list of favorite books suggested by interviewees John had as guest speakers on the episode and hit the jackpot with "Work Smarter," best seller. Nick did it, so can you with material from your podcast episodes. Give it a go. This could be your life line to running successful business online.

10. Special Events Sponsorship

"When it comes to motivating people to higher standards of performance, nothing – not even money works as powerfully as the recognition of individual effort and achievement," Patrick Lencioni said. Event organizers ride on the wings of celebrities to make a kill with podcasts.

Jerry had a great idea. He wanted to organize music performance for Nayanka Bell from West Africa in Kenya. Nayanka's songs enjoyed air play in the heydays of her music career. Jerry's idea was hijacked by event organizers who had the means.

If Jerry had the same idea today, he would be laughing all the way to bank. The bottle necks and restrictions on organizing such events would be a click of the mouse or phone call away.

When Brian was running for University secretary general post, Richard his close ally assisted with online publication to organize garbage cleaning exercise in one run down estate. This one day event saw Brian's rating soar up by 15% as potential contender for this post.

This event organization, improved Brian's image on the campaign trail. It will do the same for you in business.

Summary

Running successful online business requires more than acquired knowledge and skills. Strategic Marketing tips and techniques will sink or set your business sail into the distant future of uncharted territories. That is the emphasis throughout this chapter.

The chapter shows you how to podcast can transform your small to a vast online business empire with Six Modern Methods of Online Business Promotion and Ten Smart Ways of Making Podcast Profitable. You intend to make mileage online; podcast is a must activity to include in your business diary today.

-Chapter 8-

How to Monitor Podcast Performance Progress

Five decades ago many were amazed by the hints of exploration and achievement of early computers. Four decades down memory lane came the fascination with wartime information transmitted through radar.

It is three decades since experimental with online television and sound broadcasting became world sensation. You can't predict with reasonable accuracy what will be regarded modern technology in the next ten years. Five-to-ten year predictions on technology advancement read like science fiction today but will be out of date in the near future.

In the meantime, the use of podcast to grow online business and maximize on profit is the next big thing.

Time wasted on transit, fares, and drinks for the business executives adds up the cost to additional several hundred dollars for only an hour, two or three hour face to face meeting to show for it. The shareholders would take a dim view of these expenses, but the overall consumption of energy cannot be compensated.

These executives could stay at home, transact business through phone. It is true that the telephone is not always enough. Graphs need to be seen, little frowns have to be observed, cynical smiles say a great deal. This is where podcast comes into the picture. The world is moving away from close circuit television. And the next big thing to sitting down opposite a colleague in another city, personal dislike being what they are, is sometimes more preferable than sitting down opposite a colleague in the same room.

If your memory of teleconference is still vivid, you remember, studios into which ten executives were squeezed, five of whom televised at one time by a remotely controlled camera in the past.

Another camera was mounted over the table to zoom in on charts, documents, and models. This do-it-yourself television show provided a direct link with one, or two sets of colleagues in a studio, while a fourth and less important branch came in on sound only. You're assuming the post office has no access to the conference or takes part once the call has been set up, so there is no need to fear listening in for industrial secrets, or will the Chairperson of another company arrive on your screen via a crossed line and demand to talk to the CEO in the process.

You're wondering where this is leading. This is enthusiasm about savings made and "economy in managerial time," on the ground. Podcast is the answer. This last chapter in the book highlights benefits of podcasting with Five Future Forecasts from Tracking Podcast Content, drawing your attention to Four Mandatory Monitoring and Evaluation tools, examining Six Essential Elements for Monitoring Podcast and concludes with a brief Recap of the two significant acronyms used as the cornerstone of podcasting in this book. The two acronyms are S.C.O.P.E and P.O.D.C.A.S.T.

Six Reasons Why You should Upgrade the System

You've come a long way from concept to content creation and now the podcast is running. You've learned many lessons from challenges. You started off with basic equipment and upgraded over a period of time. Your greatest moment in podcasting came when the benefits from increased sale of product/service began to trickle in when you hit the 3000 subscribers' threshold.

Responsibilities from the volume of added new tasks in this exercise could have overcome you. You weathered the storms of blowing winds of change, adjusting where necessary, slowing down and speeding up the process from time to time staying focused on the ultimate goal. You're yet to clock the six figures, but a light is shining at the end of the tunnel beckoning you to soldier on podcasting. No surrender. No retreat, the destination, world class online business empire. Let no one talk you out it. Individuals have done it. You can do it too.

Your podcasting is no longer Return On Investment affair activity. That stage is in the past. Your eyes are set beyond breaking even in business to creating a multimillion dollar industry. You've the ticket and the plane to take you to greater heights of prosperity is podcasting. Will your podcasting plane stay on course and fly the business to the six figure destination? Yes you can and must reach that goal. What steps must you take to advance the course of your flight? Here are five things you need to consider with regard to keeping up to date with technology in the industry.

Everything is in perpetual movement including new technology to keep podcasting on fresh and fruitful topics. That calls for upgrade.

- Scale up Podcasting Process with New Technology

If you've been using the same equipment for over seven going to ten years, consider upgrading the equipment. You need fast speed in a rapidly changing world of information exchange. Upgrading gets your computer to boot fast, and run well with the latest software. You also save time, energy in creating content and transmission to desired destination for broadcast is fast.

- Secure Suitable Software Solution

What software are you using now? If your computer is still running on XP you're years behind. But that is not all. The worst is yet to come when the manufacturers- Microsoft discontinues making support software for XP. That is not in the distant.

It is not long when CDs replaced diskettes. It has not taken time for CDs to fade in the background. It won't take time when new technology comes into existence to replace what is trending. The secret is to keep up with technology upgrade. Skype is enjoying immense online communication popularity but new entrants in the market are making inroads. You love and use Skype, but don't close the door to other forms of online communication to keep in touch with your target audience. ,

- Save Time

No one has more minutes to the hour, hours to the day. You've an equal share of time with the competitor. The difference is in how you use your time wisely or wastefully. How much time do you spend to put together material for an episode of video podcast? The duration of time you take says a lot about how you spend your time.

How about mundane activities such as tea breaks, telephone calls not related to productive work activities? You could be throwing away valuable time without realizing until you sit down with a pen and paper and map out your day's activity. You'll be surprised how much free time you've on hand to channel into productive course such as podcasting.

- Speed up the Process

Modern technology is designed to save time and give you maximum results. Tips and techniques of doing things fast and effectively are available if you look around. You could be lagging behind in correspondence simply because you've not discovered that Outlook 2016 with a "smart inbox," will get you on top of backlog email correspondence in no time.

Widen the scope and ability of computer use with the latest software that is also compatible with Smartphone in the market today.

- Self Employment is no longer frowned upon.

Thanks to the internet. Podcasting is all about Do-It-Yourself. Self set up and launch without outside assistance. How easy could the process be? What could be better than picking and purchasing the right equipment, setting and launching the podcast alone?

It gets better. You end up running the podcast from the comfort of your home and convenience of your house and earning a descent living from all these efforts without moving out of the house, paying office rent, wrestling with the car to beat the traffic jam down town. You save the best for last doing what you love to do best.

- Share Information

You've worked hard at every stage of putting together podcast and creating content which is at the heart beat of this whole exercise. But if no one else except you gets to share the information, it's not worth the effort. In line with the definition of communication podcasting is sharing thoughts, opinions and ideas with the target audience. WordPress blog allows you to share articles with friends instantly. You're then able to monitor and evaluate the outcome.

Monitoring and Evaluation Tools

Rhodri, CEO of Plastic Plant Company set up production unit to manufacture and sell plastic containers at wholesale and retail. In seven months of operation, the demand outstripped production. The company had pending orders of up to three months to supply consumers. The CEO convened a special management stuff meeting consisting of lower, middle and top management representatives to map out a strategy in meeting this growing demand.

The meeting resolved to introduce night shift to adjust and cope with the demand on production unit. Part time employees were recruited to work under supervision of permanent staff members on night duty. This project ran on well with huge turn over profit margin for seven months before the company started to realize cracks in the system accrued from overtime payments.

Production line fell below expectation but the company paid out money commensurate with time clocked. The foreman of the plant was tasked to ensure no one slept on the job. But, he was not able to be at the plant every night to check on production activities. The company was forced to install CCTV to monitor work progress in the absence of human supervision. Seven cameras were secretly installed concealed to pick up and record the activities and progress of the work at night. Rhodri discovered that night shift staff got paid yet slept on the job most of the time at night.

Monitoring progress does not need to be elaborate as in this case of employees sleeping on the job. But it is important to have checks and balances to gauge business progress. If your podcast is not yielding expected business projections, make adjustments in areas of weakness to put more efforts on areas of strong strength for the business to meet its overall objectives.

Monitoring and evaluation are important tools for measuring gains and accomplishments made in business and different activities. You don't have to be a mathematical whiz to get and use facts and figures from these tools to enable you develop superior quality content your customers and subscribers need.

You want to know how the business is doing now and its future expansion prospects to moderate podcast activities. Positive response is welcome anytime. You should also welcome negative reactions. It is not so much your reaction as it is the action you take to remedy the situation in the event of negative results from monitoring and evaluation.

Use positive results to strengthen areas of strength. Negative results are not necessarily a sign of weakness of content on your part. A number of issues could precipitate and lead to poor performance. That is why it is important to scrutinize the result and not take it at face value without giving it due consideration to locate and identify the cause. Go beyond the symptoms to root out the real problem and get value from these two tools. How do you go about the process?

- Regular Podcast Reviews

In an organization, reviews bring together different management level staff members t to deliberate on the institution's vision and mission statements. Individual podcaster only has monitoring and evaluation tools for progress report verification.

Make no mistake. Results reflect the activities of the institution and individual whether good or bad. Take heart. Numbers give strength in institution but cannot influence and alter the outcome of monitoring and evaluation.

- Reality Check on Personality

Individual contribution make up institution framework in carrying out different tasks aimed at producing the same result to grow the business. Keep up to date with regular reviews. Whether you're using multiple platforms or one, your work is cut out to attain set goals.

You engage guest bloggers, but the responsibility and outcome of the podcast rests on your shoulders. Talents come and go as in stage drama acting. You're the floor manager, the main actor, props organizer and everything else that goes into making drama a success. Liken this scenario to podcasting.

You're the technical personnel to set up and launch the activity, create and present content, the time keeper, the financial controller and whatever activities you perform to run your podcast. It will cost you dearly if you ignore reality check on personality.

Section one, chapter one opens with superior qualities of a successful podcaster. Chapter four gives additional Five Personality Traits which Influence Successful Marketing Strategy Outcome.

This concluding chapter in the book revisits the topic on personality by stressing on paying attention to personality of the person of the moment. Here, the consideration on personality revolves around your frequency and regularity on performance of the activities.

- Frequency of Involvement

What is holding you back from realizing your full potential in podcasting? You need to closely examine results from feedback generated out of monitoring and evaluation. Zero in and deal with one item after the other.

For example, you recently started a radio talk show on the side and the program has brought in encouraging feedback results. That means more work on your part. The radio talk show could eat into your content preparation time for the blog post. Address the issue with an open mind keeping the main purpose in sharp view. Do you need to make more time and concentrate on the radio talk show? How will the radio show influence podcasting results? These and other questions should give you direction and guidance in decision making.

- Regularity of Check Ins

What do you need to speed up the process? Suppose the results of monitoring show overwhelming demand for instant article on Face Book. You might want to reorganize your priorities to accommodate and maximize on the strength of this channel of communication. This leads to asking questions to cope with feedback from the channel.

- How frequent should you attend to respondents of instant articles?

- Do you need an extra hand to handle the correspondence?

- How does it affect the overall goal of podcasting?

This is your show. You started it from scratch. You've great expectations for future expansion of the business. Look inside for the hero within to take you through the hustle and bustle of maintaining consistency in producing quality content for the format you've chosen - audio or video.

You might want to rearrange the original priority to include emerging issues to stay on course and on top of the game as you keep eyes fixed on the ultimate price to monetize podcast using five essential elements.

Five Future Forecasts from Tracking Podcast Content

In each of the previous six chapters, there is constant mention of content leaving no doubt, content is the corner stone without which the foundation of this exercise would crumble. What constitutes good content? How do you go about producing compelling content? These questions are answered in details in the book.

"If it ain't broke, why fix it, "Henry Ford said. It has taken you time to set up and launch your podcast and its running, so why tinker with it. This is a valid question to ask if you've spent time, energy and resources in the process to ensure you're up and running. Specific to this chapter, you'll learn how to turn on full lights on podcasting beyond set up and launch to charm the customer to take action.

You've put in place measures to ensure every step of podcasting meets set goals. How do you track the success of content, marketing strategy, monetizing podcast among other activities in running the show?

Your yardstick for measurement is unique to the podcast and person behind it. You need to monitor every aspect as indeed you've from set up to launching. Now that your podcast is up running, the challenge is to stay focused and consistent to deliver on promise. Here are five areas to pay attention to in this process.

- Review Content Posted on Different Platforms

Review set up, content material from time to time. Start now by going over content you've published in different platforms. Sort and arrange them in order of titles, dates, and channels. Set up a working system which allows you access to information in the past, present and prospective future. This system should come handy in tracking progress performance. You get to learn how the blog post, instant articles on Face Book and other social media outlets are doing.

- Resolve Platform Information

Resolve the amount of information you need to collect from different platforms and posts. This way you're not bogged down going over entire materials. This could be time consuming. You gain insight by gleaning on past, present and future topics on the subject. Here are three things to consider with regard to different posts.

- You use guest bloggers, talents in the show. Go over and discover how their contribution matches yours and the goal of podcasting.

- Track audio/video, blog posts formats separately if you're on multiple formats.

- Sort out posts in categories to make tracking content in each category easy. You learn what interests your customers most from feedback. This helps to refine the topic, give it a new spin and repurpose it for a different format.

- Renew Your Resolve

Whatever kind of measurement you use should give you insight on content, platform format to achieve the business objectives. Compare and contrast blog posts with social media to get a glimpse of subscribers' action from feedback on the post. Don't be content with mere "likes," on Face Book, dig deeper for more information to improve your serve.

- Rating Revelations

Rate content performances in tangible numbers say 1-10, then work out the average to give you an overview of progress across the board. This way you're able to focus on the average of a given platform to make necessary adjustments for improvement. You could also use colors to survey different podcast formats and platforms.

You want to know the average number of emails from your blog post, use green for posts attracting five and above score and red for below that number. The duration of tracking depends on posting frequency. If you post monthly, that determines when to track previous content.

- Regulate Tracking to Match Posting Frequency

Time in between posting, publishing and response from subscribers is a good barometer to draw conclusions on best practices. Sure you need to keep abreast with each posting performance. However, make time to gather information over designated period of time to enable you get a good picture of the exercise from figures and facts.

Whether you're running individual or institution podcast, the ultimate goal is to use results to expand quality of content in subsequent podcast episodes.

Summary

When it comes to reaching a large audience online to promote your product/service, nothing works fast and effective in favor of your business as peak performance in offering quality content. This last chapter walks you through Five Future Forecasts from Tracking Podcast Content, Four Mandatory Monitoring and Evaluation Tools and concludes with Five Essential Elements for Monetizing Podcast. All aboard, your podcast plane is ready to take off and all eyes are on you as the pilot.

Acronyms

G.I.G.O in computer language represents "Garbage In, Garbage Out."

S.C.O.P.E. stands for:-

        S – Speed.

        C – Control/Convenience.

        O – Organization.

        P – Period/Duration of Time. .

        E – Economic Value.

And P.O.D.D.C.A.S.T stands for

        P- Planning

        O - Organization

        D - Directing

        C - Controlling

        A - Asking and Answering Questions

        S - Structure and Format

        T - Techniques

Resources/References

- 7 Tips for Launching a Successful Podcast - http://mashable.com/2011/03/25/podcasting-tips/#1Sv6jMWJXSqa

- 19 Ways To Monetize Your Podcast - http://rachelrofe.com/19-ways-to-monetize-your-podcast

- Are You Getting the Most Out of Social Media Marketing? - https://www.allbusiness.com/getting-most-out-of-social-media-marketing-105086-1.htm

- Monitoring and Tracking Methods - http://virtualnotdistant.com/monitoring-progress-and-tracking-results-1/

- 4 Step Process for Creating Compelling Content for Your Audience - http://www.marketingprofs.com/articles/2016/29307/a-four-step-process-for-creating-compelling-content-for-your-audience#ixzz47zlzlkzm

6. Effective Content Marketing: 5 Steps to Track Your Efforts -

http://contentmarketinginstitute.com/2014/07/effective-content-marketing-track-efforts/

- 4 Tips to Improve Your Social Media Exposure - http://www.socialmediaexaminer.com/4-tips-to-improve-your-pinterest-exposure/?awt_l=PYMklw&

- 10 Tips for Adding Video to Your Digital Marketing Mix-Video-Marketing-Tips-IBM.pdf

- How to Create Quality Facebook Canvas Ads -http://www.socialmediaexaminer.com/how-to-create-quality-facebook-canvas-ads/?awt_l=PYMklw&awt_m=3dJPxjX9pcr.ILT

10. Virtual Reality Is Finally Here—Is Your Business Ready to Benefit From It? -

https://www.allbusiness.com/virtual-reality-is-finally-here-is-your-business-ready-to-benefit-104165-1.html?utm_source=getresponse&utm_medium=email&utm_campaign=allbusiness&utm_ntent=Avoid+These+Time+Wasters+|+Weekly+Roundup+April+23rd

Get your copy of this e-book online today!